Taxes for RV Owners

Taxes for RV Owners

What every full-time RVer should know about taxes

HEATHER RYAN, EA

Heather Ryan, EA

tax-queen.com

Contents

Part I. Tax Considerations for all RVers

Part II. Tax Considerations for Nomad Owned Businesses

Part III. How to Handle Taxes When Renting Out Your RV or Home

Part IV. 2018 Tax Reform

Notes from the Author

I'm Heather Ryan and I've been on the road full-time in an RV with my husband and two dogs since September 2016. As a full-time traveler, I understand many of the unique tax situations of nomads. I also fully support entrepreneurs and the struggles they face.

I am the owner of Tax Queen, a tax accounting and bookkeeping firm focused on helping small business entrepreneurs. I can help with both business and personal returns. With over 10 years of bookkeeping experience, I am here to support you in any way I can.

Little known facts about me. I hold a degree in computer science from Tufts University and have spent years working in professional kitchens after attending Johnson & Wales University for baking and pastry arts. Lastly, I used to own a specialty baking business creating allergy-free wedding and specialty cakes.

Now you're thinking what qualifies me to help with your bookkeeping and taxes?

I have spent many years helping different businesses with their bookkeeping, establishing solid financial structures and cleaning up their books for tax purposes. I am a QuickBooks Certified ProAdvisor and understand what it means to be financially organized.

After several years working under an Enrolled Agent to better understand taxes, she passed her clients to me to allow for her retirement. I have continued to further my studies and am now an Enrolled Agent myself.

Enrolled Agent (EA) is the highest credential the IRS awards.

EAs are federally licensed in the field of taxation with unlimited practice rights before the IRS. This means I am not restricted by state lines as to which taxpayers I can represent. I can handle any tax matter and represent a taxpayer before any IRS office.

As an entrepreneur myself, I can relate to the challenges you face as a small business owner. I also understand that many small business owners dislike, or are confused by, the accounting side of things. That is where I shine. I enjoy learning about a business and seeing how I can help that business succeed, whether that's through better financial organization or tax savings.

I offer personal attention and services for each individual client. My services are completely location independent, so I can help people that live the life of freedom via a secure client portal, email, and phone.

If you are ready to learn more about what I can do for you, I encourage you to contact me.

What inspired me to write this book?

I surround myself with entrepreneurs. My grandparents were small business owners, my father was an entrepreneur and now, my husband is one. I'm always meeting new people on the road who have amazingly creative businesses and ideas. As a full-time traveler, I see the struggle with taxes as a nomad is real and common.

I was already writing blog posts for Tax-Queen.com to address some of these questions when Heath Padgett asked to interview me for The RV Entrepreneur Podcast. After this interview, I realized how many questions people had about taxes for those who live an itinerant life. Plus, it can be so confusing to know what can and cannot be expensed as a small business owner. By answering Heath's questions and seeing all the knowledge I had to bring to the table, I knew I could help others ease the struggle.

With the writing of this book, I'm hoping to clarify many tax and business-related terms that may be confusing or are oftentimes misunderstood.

Whether you are just getting started as a business owner or you struggle to know what can and cannot be deductible as an RVer, this book is for you. It is here to help you navigate terms and make it easier for you to understand tax obligations and deductions.

Dig in!

Heather Ryan

Introduction

Do any of the following statements resonate with you?

You're an entrepreneur.

You own or want to start a small business.

You live on the road in an RV or van or are a nomad of some sort.

You are confused about your taxes now that you live on the road.

You own a small business, but don't know what expenses you can take on your taxes.

You're not alone. These things overwhelm and confuse many full-time RV owners. There's so much to learn and understand.

Let's get started.

PART I
TAX CONSIDERATIONS FOR ALL RVERS

Regardless of whether you have a business on the road, there are credits and other things to consider. While you may not always qualify for larger tax credits, think of the life you are living.

This is your dream, right?

The freedom to travel and experience this beautiful country is a pretty awesome thing and one that should not be overlooked even if you don't qualify for extra credits.

1. Domicile

Domicile: a common word used for full-time travelers or nomads, but what does it mean? Why is it important?

Simply put, your domicile is your home state — the one state you consider your permanent place of residence. You can have more than one physical home, but only one domicile (i.e., a vacation home in one state and your permanent home in another).

Some factors that indicate where you're domiciled include where you vote, register your car/RV, and receive legal mail. Domicile is fundamentally a question of your intent. Which state do you consider your permanent home?

RV Domicile and Residency

As an RVer, your domicile is the place you intend to live once you're done traveling. Even if your travels never come to an end, or you eventually move to a new state, that's okay. While you're traveling, your domicile is, for all intents and purposes, where you intend to live.

In short, your domicile is your home state. You use your domicile as your legal address. You file taxes with that address, register your vehicles in that state, get auto insurance rates based on that address, and have a driver's license that reflects that state. Even though you might not physically live in your domicile state, it is your home or residence state. With your RV you might reside in many states over the course of a year, but your legal address is still your domicile.

As an example, I'll share my own situation. When I first started full-time RVing, we were residents or domiciled in Colorado. We had a sticks-and-bricks home there. We had Colorado driver's licenses and Colorado license plates. We voted there and paid Colorado state income taxes. Then we "moved" to Florida. We didn't physically buy a house there or rent an apartment, but we did get a legal address there. We declared it our domicile with the county office. We registered our 5th wheel and truck there. We now file our taxes with our Florida address. We are officially Floridians, our new domicile state.

Why is understanding domicile important?

Your domicile is the address you'll use to file your taxes. If your domicile state has a state income tax, be prepared to pay it. Choosing a state with no income tax could be quite beneficial for many reasons, but keep in mind under certain scenarios you might still owe another state an income tax return and possibly taxes.

That's right.

If you physically work in a state where you are employed as a workamper or camp host, or if you conduct physical business in multiple states, you may owe state income tax to other states even if your domicile state doesn't have an income tax. Let's not worry too much about this right now, especially if you're just getting started. I'll dive further into this in Chapter 4.

2. Solar Credit: Don't Miss Out!

This year is different because **this was the year you installed solar on your RV** (or qualifying home), and now you're ready to get that big fat tax credit to take 30% right off the top of that expense. I'm here to hopefully clarify this process.

If you're reading this and haven't yet installed solar on your RV, you only have one more year to get this sweet tax credit. 30% off the cost of a system is nothing to scoff at people, but the tax credit decreases to 26% for tax year 2020; drops to 22% for tax year 2021; then expires December 31, 2021... so what are you waiting for?

Yes. Your RV or motorhome qualifies for this residential energy tax credit!

Now then, let's get down to it.

What you need to claim the tax credit

1. The receipts for your solar installation. I always push for keeping good records. (You'll notice this is a running theme in this book.)
2. IRS Form 1040
3. IRS Schedule 3 as part of Form 1040
4. IRS Form 5695

What qualifies as residential energy property?

Taken directly from the IRS:

> Include any labor costs properly allocable to the onsite preparation, assembly, or original installation of the residential energy efficient property and for piping or wiring to interconnect such property to the home.
>
> Qualified solar electric property costs are costs for property that uses solar energy to generate electricity for use in your home located in the United States. No costs relating to a solar panel or other property installed as a roof (or portion thereof) will fail to qualify solely because the property constitutes a structural component of the structure on which it is installed. The home does not have to be your main home.

All of that is a fancy way of saying pretty much any cost related to installation and materials counts. Claim it. This includes a battery, inverter, wiring, and labor to install.

Form 5695 – Taking the credit

The thing about the solar tax credit is that it isn't "fully refundable," meaning you can only take a credit for what you owe in taxes. This is different than other fully refundable tax credits, such as the Child Tax Credit and Earned Income Tax Credit.

Luckily, you can carry over the unused credit to the next tax year. For example, if you were not able to claim the whole credit on your 2019 taxes, you get to reduce your 2020 tax bill, too. A tax liability calculation worksheet is provided in the instructions for Form 5695.

This allows you to add up your tax credits to see how much you qualify to take on the residential energy tax credit.

Form 1040 Schedule 3 Line 53

Below is an example of how your credit amount will show up on Form 1040. If your solar energy system cost you $16,000, your taxes are reduced by a credit of $4,800. However, if you only have a tax obligation of $4,600, that's all the credit you can claim for that tax year. You can carry the other $200 credit over to the next tax year.

SCHEDULE 3 (Form 1040)	Nonrefundable Credits	OMB No. 1545-0074 2018
Department of the Treasury Internal Revenue Service	▶ Attach to Form 1040. ▶ Go to www.irs.gov/Form1040 for instructions and the latest information.	Attachment Sequence No. 03
Name(s) shown on Form 1040		Your social security number

Nonrefundable Credits			
	48	Foreign tax credit. Attach Form 1116 if required	48	
	49	Credit for child and dependent care expenses. Attach Form 2441	49	
	50	Education credits from Form 8863, line 19	50	
	51	Retirement savings contributions credit. Attach Form 8880	51	
	52	Reserved	52	
	53	Residential energy credit. Attach Form 5695	53	4,800
	54	Other credits from Form a ☐ 3800 b ☐ 8801 c ☐	54	
	55	Add the amounts in the far right column. Enter here and include on Form 1040, line 12	55	4,800

For Paperwork Reduction Act Notice, see your tax return instructions. BEA Schedule 3 (Form 1040) 2018

Frequently Asked Questions Regarding Solar

Should I claim the tax credit if I partially paid (e.g., a deposit) this year for an installation that won't be completed until the following year?

No. The instructions for Form 5695 explicitly state that costs are treated as paid when the original installation of the item is complete. Therefore, you can claim all the costs for your installation no matter when they were paid, but you must wait to claim them in the year the installation is complete. Keep all of your receipts and documents related to the installation!

If I installed a solar panel system a few years ago and now I want to add new panels, can I claim the credit?

Yes! You can claim the credit for any new costs associated with the addition. You can't go back and claim the credit for the previously installed equipment. Hopefully you already claimed the credit for those costs back then. However, you must install new panels to be able to take this credit. If you simply want to add more batteries to your system, I suggest adding a new panel as well to take advantage of this credit.

If I install solar and claim the tax credit, will I have to repay the credit to the government if I sell the house within a certain number of years?

No! If you install a solar panel system on a home (an RV qualifies as a home) you own, you can claim the whole credit and sell at any point afterwards. Keep in mind this is only true for homeowners, including RV owners. The law is significantly more complex for commercial solar installations.

3. Itemize or Take the Standard Deduction?

How do you know if you should itemize or take the standard deduction? First of all, what is the difference?

The standard deduction is a fixed dollar amount that reduces your taxable income and varies according to your filing status. On the other hand, itemized deductions are made up of a list of eligible expenses. You can claim whichever lowers your tax bill the most.

In my experience, a full-time RVer does not usually have enough expenses to itemize. However, there are exceptions, so you should do what is best for your situation.

Itemize or take the standard deduction?

It's a question many ask and don't understand. Here are a few tips to give you an understanding and figure out if you qualify or not. Don't forget to make sure to file the right form for your situation. Remember, all taxpayers should keep a copy of their tax return and any supporting documentation including itemized deductions.

Standard deduction rates for 2019:

If a taxpayer doesn't itemize, then the basic standard deduction for 2019 depends on your filing status. If the taxpayer is:

Single – $12,200
Married Filing Jointly – $24,400
Head of Household – $18,350

If a taxpayer is 65 or older, or blind, the standard deduction is higher than the previous amounts. For 2019, the additional standard deduction amount for those over 65 or the blind is $1,300. The deduction is limited if the taxpayer can be claimed as a dependent on someone else's return.

Figure Your Itemized Deductions:

Taxpayers need to add up deductible expenses they paid during the tax year. If these expenses are larger than your standard deduction rate, then you can itemize and get a larger deduction on your federal income tax.

These may include expenses such as:

- Home mortgage interest (can include your RV loan interest, if any)
- State and local income taxes OR sales taxes (but not both), real estate taxes and personal property taxes (taxes on vehicles are personal property). Make sure to keep receipts for larger items like an RV purchased in a tax year. Higher cost items like an RV or auto might make your sales tax greater than income tax in that year. **Beginning in 2018 and continuing in 2019, this total is limited to $10,000.**
- Gifts to charities (cash, goods, and mileage) – Make sure you have receipts. In 2019, the charity mileage rate is $0.14.
- Casualty or theft losses (only available for federally declared disaster areas starting in 2018)
- Unreimbursed medical expenses – This includes co-pays for dentists, doctors, hospital visits, medical equipment, prescription medications and even mileage to and from a doctor's office. The medical mileage rate for 2019 is $0.20.

- Unreimbursed employee business expenses – This includes travel expenses, mileage, union dues, uniform costs and more. (This provision was removed with the Tax Cuts and Jobs Act for tax years 2018-2025.)

Special rules and limits apply. Talk to your tax professional to learn more about your unique situation.

Check for Exceptions:

Married Filing Separate is the biggest exception. The law does not allow a person to claim the standard deduction if one spouse itemizes. In this case, the taxpayer's standard deduction is zero and they should itemize any deductions. See your tax professional for help on this.

4. Do I Have to File State Income Taxes?

This is a loaded question with way more than one answer. Let's first take a look to determine if you are employed in a state or are simply visiting a state and conducting business from your home.

Employed in a state

If you're employed in a state, then you are most likely going to work every day as required by your employer. This could be anything from a traveling nurse to a traveling construction worker to a campground host. This means you are physically working in that state and more than likely staying there for months at a time.

If you are employed in a state, you will owe state income taxes to that state on any income from the job completed in that state. This means if you work as a traveling nurse and earned 3 months of income in Idaho, then you owe the state of Idaho income tax on that 3 months of income.

Keep in mind, every state has a minimum income level earned before state taxes would be owed. This is where it can get complicated. However, if your employer withholds state taxes from your W-2, then you'll definitely want to file in that state. If you don't meet the minimum for paying income taxes in that state, you'll receive any taxes paid as a refund. Yes, this adds a little extra work to your tax preparation, but it's worth it to get any refund owed to you.

Let's look at an example.

You spend the summer in Colorado working as a campground host. You are paid W-2 wages and Colorado income tax is withheld. Therefore, you'll need to file a Colorado state income tax return as a nonresident.

Directly from the state of Colorado:

> A nonresident is an individual who did not reside within the boundaries of Colorado at any time during the tax year. However, the person may have temporarily lived and/or worked in Colorado. A nonresident is required to file a Colorado income tax return if they:
>
> - are required to file a federal income tax return, and
> - had taxable Colorado-source income.
>
> Nonresidents will initially determine their Colorado taxable income as though they are full-year residents. Nonresidents of Colorado will complete the Colorado Individual Income Tax Booklet DR 0104 and the Nonresident tax calculation schedule DR 0104PN to determine what income will be claimed on the Colorado 104 return.

You can see it gets complicated, and you need to understand the law for any state in which you physically worked and earned income was reported on a W-2.

Let's go into a little more detail about the different types of income earned for being an employee (W-2 wage earner) vs. contractor (1099-Misc) because it deserves a little attention and explanation.

1099-Misc vs. W-2 Wages

If you workamp or work any job helping someone else's

business, it's important to know the difference between being an employee vs. being a contractor.

First off, an employee receives a W-2 while a contractor receives a 1099-Misc. Typically, if you receive a 1099-Misc as a contractor, you are self-employed. Being self-employed comes with several additional complications when filing taxes and it also means you'll most likely need to pay self-employment taxes on that income.

Remember, the IRS has factors to determine who is an employee and who is an independent contractor, so as to collect the right amount of payroll taxes. The primary factor is the "degree of control" the employer has over the employee. In other words, if you're required to work 9-5 every day, you're an employee.

However, there are advantages that come with being an employee. For starters, your employer must pay for half of the payroll taxes which includes Social Security and Medicare taxes). If you're an independent contractor, you're on the hook for paying the full 15.3% of Social Security and Medicare tax up to the Social Security wage base ($132,900 in 2019), and then the full 2.9% on income above that threshold.

In addition, employees are eligible for a host of fringe benefits that many times are provided by an employer. Health insurance and retirement plans are two great examples. Before you go rushing off to become an independent contractor to save some dough, you've got to consider these factors.

If you receive a 1099-Misc from the place where you were working, then you are self-employed and have your own business. This means you can take deductions from income of any business expenses, and you need to file a Schedule C as part of your 1040. I discuss business expenses in a whole section about Taxes for Nomad Owned Businesses. If you're a new business owner, then make sure you read through that section to get a better understanding of any possible tax deductions that you may qualify for.

Other situations where you might owe multiple state income tax returns

Now that you understand receiving W-2 wages in a state, let's look at other situations.

A great example of owing multiple state returns is doing craft shows or art festivals. This means you travel to different states and earn income in each of those states while working a weekend art show. Technically, you might owe income tax to that state for any income earned while physically selling goods there.

You can see where this can get complicated and also quite expensive when there is a need to file a tax return in so many states. I know of certain states that consider that you are working in that state the minute you set up shop there, while others give allowances for transient workers. It's important to know the rules for the various states to which you will travel.

I will end here and suggest you talk with a tax expert about your individual situation because of the differences described above.

PART II
TAX CONSIDERATIONS FOR NOMAD OWNED BUSINESSES

Taxes – nobody likes them, but we all must pay them, right? Now that your business is nomadic, let's look at what is deductible and what is not. Deductions can vary from a stationary life, so be extra careful here.

Living in an RV definitely takes away some deductions, but then consider the freedom you have running a business that is completely location independent. These pluses make up for those lost deductions, right?!?

In my eyes, the nomadic lifestyle is worth the loss of a few tax deductions.

In any case, you're here to learn what you can deduct, so let's get to explaining.

What are deductible expenses?

To be deductible, a business expense must be both "ordinary and necessary." An ordinary expense is one that is common and accepted in your trade or business. A necessary expense is one that is helpful and appropriate to conduct your business. An expense does not have to be essential to be considered necessary.

Ordinary business expenses

First things first. You can deduct ordinary business expenses including costs of goods sold, office supplies, small equipment, postage, software subscription services, bank charges, credit card fees, interest charges, business insurance and more.

Your business might have a special category related to your trade and that's ok. Make sure that your records are clearly represented by keeping all receipts that show your expenses.

Now let's get into specific expenses which should help clarify some of the big questions.

5. Auto Expenses and Deductions

This is a big topic for full-time RVers and one that doesn't have one right answer. The following will help you determine how to best deduct any mileage for the business use of your vehicle.

Can I write-off all my RV mileage?

As a small business owner, you can claim expenses related to the business use of your vehicle on your federal income tax return in one of two ways:

1. Use the standard mileage deduction
2. Deduct the actual car expenses

To use the standard mileage rate at all, you must use it the first year you use the vehicle for business.

However, in later years, you can switch from the standard mileage rate to the actual expenses method. If you change to the actual expenses method in a later year, but before your car is fully depreciated, you need to know the remaining useful life of the car and use straight line depreciation. If you don't know what I'm talking about here with depreciation, I cover this in Chapter 8. For now, it's more important to understand what needs to happen

If you lease a vehicle and want to use the standard mileage rate, you must use the standard mileage rate for the entire lease period.

Let's dig further into the two methods.

Standard Mileage

When computing your deduction using the standard mileage, you'll take the miles driven and multiply that times the IRS standard mileage rate (which for 2019 is 58 cents). It's good to note that the standard mileage rate changes yearly. It's more important to know the miles because most tax software will calculate the amount for you.

You don't need to calculate the deduction for each drive. Instead, keep track of the total business miles for the year. When you complete your taxes, give your tax advisor the beginning of year mileage, business mileage, personal mileage, and end of year mileage. To get the deduction, the total business miles will be multiplied by the standard mileage rate. Again, most tax software will compute this for you once you enter in the miles driven for business.

For example, if you drove 1,000 miles for business during the year, you'd take

1,000 x .58 to get a business deduction of $580

Actual Expenses

If you use your car for both business and personal purposes, you must divide your expenses between business and personal use. You will divide your vehicle deduction based on the miles driven for each purpose. In order to take actual expenses, you'll need to record all expenses related to the vehicle including mileage, maintenance, insurance, registration costs, etc.

When you take actual expenses, you can take depreciation for the vehicle based on business use percentage. However, if you sell that vehicle, you may need to repay the depreciation on the vehicle sale. This is called depreciation recapture. Once again, I go into further detail about depreciation in Chapter 8.

Make sure to keep good records of all maintenance,

insurance, total vehicle mileage, miles for personal use, etc. With this method, you'll be able to use a percentage of those expenses, based on your business use of the vehicle, as a tax deduction. I illustrate this with an example below.

Standard Mileage vs. Actual Expenses: Which is better?

Typically, I find the standard mileage rate easier (less record keeping needed) and more cost effective than actual expenses. However, you can keep all receipts related to your auto (oil changes, insurance costs, registration fees, etc.) and run the numbers at the end of the year to determine which is the most cost effective for you. Remember, to be eligible to use the standard mileage rate at all, you must use it the first year you use the vehicle for business.

You'll want to remember to record the beginning of year mileage so that you can determine the total annual mileage for your vehicle. If you have an auto loan or registration costs, you need the percentage of business use in order to take those expenses.

For example, your car started at 30,000 miles on January 1, 2019. On January 1, 2020, its odometer reads 45,000. You know you've driven 15,000 for the year 2019. You have recorded 5,000 miles for the business. This means 30% of the miles driven were for business purposes. You also paid $3,000 in interest on your auto loan.

To illustrate the above deduction, here is a sample worksheet:

Beginning Mileage	30000	Business % Use	33.33%
End Mileage	45000		
Total Mileage	15000	Auto Loan Interest	3000
		Auto Maintenance	500
		Property Tax	275
Total Business Miles	5000	Total Expenses	6775
Total Mileage Deduction	$2,700		
Total Mileage Deduction with standard deduction	$2,900	Total Actual Expenses Deduction for business use of vehicle	$2,258

Sole Proprietor

As a sole proprietor, you can deduct mileage for running business errands like going to the bank or the post office.

Miles driven can also include miles to and from a business location or a business meeting over lunch. Say you have to visit a client's office or are doing a photo shoot on site. These count as business miles. You'll most likely be using your car or truck for these miles, so make sure to keep documentation or a written log. Your log should include the date, business purpose (who you met with and why), mileage total and mileage at the start of the year.

There are also some great apps out there to help keep track of mileage. MileIQ is one of my favorites, along with Expensify and Milog. I do offer a discount for getting a paid unlimited drive plan with MileIQ (you must use this link to get the discount https://bit.ly/2pywqEs). MileIQ offers a free plan for 40 drives/month.

You can also keep a simple spreadsheet with this data, or maybe a handwritten notebook kept in your car or truck works better for you. I usually stress a digital copy, so that you have backups should paper get lost or destroyed. Use what you're comfortable with and what you know you will keep up with. If that means a notebook in the car, then go for it. If using an app on your phone means you'll keep it up-to-date, then go that route.

All I truly stress is keeping good records. (I told you already this would be a running theme, right?)

S Corporation and Partnerships

If you have an S corporation (S corp) or partnership and have business-related expenses that you pay for with a personal credit card or checking account, then you need to implement an accountable plan. Under an accountable plan, a business reimburses its employees to cover business expenses incurred including meals, travel, entertainment, mileage, etc.

As a partnership in a partnership, it is legitimate to reimburse a partner for business expenses paid with a personal credit card or bank account. It's important to keep good records of what the reimbursements were for (receipts are needed) and also to make sure the reimbursement gets recorded on the books accurately.

With an S corp, YOU are an employee of your own company. Receiving W-2 wages from your own S corp is an IRS requirement, so treat yourself like any other employee and create an accountable plan.

I encourage business owners to implement an accountable plan to reimburse an employee (can be you or any employee) for any expenses that are mixed used (both personal and business) like cell phone, mileage or internet costs. This is where you could get reimbursed personally for a home office deduction as an S corp if it applies to your personal situation.

Accountable Plan

One of the rules for an accountable plan is that you must adequately account for any expenses. This means you must keep good records of all expenses including receipts for all business expenses. There it is again, good record keeping – the running theme in this book.

If the IRS questions a deduction on your return, these supporting documents are what you would need to provide to the IRS to prove legitimate business expenses.

Taken directly from the IRS website:

> To be an accountable plan, your employer's reimbursement or allowance arrangement must include all of the following rules.
>
> - Your expenses must have a business connection — that is, you must have paid or incurred deductible expenses while performing services as an employee of your employer.
> - You must adequately account to your employer for these expenses within a reasonable period of time.
> - You must return any excess reimbursement or allowance within a reasonable period of time.
>
> An excess reimbursement or allowance is any amount you are paid that is more than the business-related expenses that you adequately accounted for to your employer.

Per Diem for S Corp

If you're trying to keep things simple, the IRS allows the use of per diem rates for travel and incidental expenses. A per diem rate is the equivalent of a fixed amount paid to an employee to compensate for lodging, meals, and incidental expenses incurred when traveling for business purposes.

These rates vary according to geographic location. Using per diem rates, a business can deduct the payment as an expense, but the employee does not get this amount added to wages.

The U.S. General Services Administration (GSA) sets per diem rates, so you'll want to check their website (https://www.gsa.gov/travel-resources) for the rates for specific locations. If you pay an employee more than the per diem rate for that area, then the difference is considered wages and is taxable to the employee.

Keep in mind, travel expenses are deductible only if they are considered ordinary and necessary business expenses for traveling away from home. I'll go into more detail about tax home later, so look for it if you think it applies to you.

Remember that you cannot deduct expenses eligible for reimbursement under an employer accountable plan – even if you did not claim the reimbursement. The provision that used to allow you to deduct actual expenses which exceeded the per diem rate was removed as part of the Tax Cuts and Jobs Act for years 2018-2025. This means employee business expenses are no longer part of itemized deductions.

Lastly, to be paid per diem rates, an employee must provide an expense report to show all costs incurred. Without a complete report, per diem payments are taxable to the employee.

This is the same requirement if an employee is reimbursed for actual expenses except, in this case, the employee receives a flat amount for each day of travel.

In a nutshell, a per diem rate can be used by an employer to reimburse employees for combined lodging, incidental and meal costs. Those per diem payments are not considered part of the employee's wages for tax purposes as long as the payments are equal to or less than the federal per diem rate and the employee provides a complete expense report. If there's no expense report, payments are taxable to that employee. Similarly, any payments which are more than the per diem rate will also be taxable.

If you're still confused, the IRS put together a worksheet (https://www.irs.gov/pub/irs-regs/perdiemfaq&a.prn.pdf) to help explain per diem.

Should my company buy my car/truck?

This is a complicated question with several key factors to consider for your situation and business.

Let's go over some things to consider when a company owns a vehicle.

First, if the company owns the vehicle, it needs to have a title in the company's name. This means the company needs to hold the loan or lease. It isn't always easy for a new company with no credit history to secure a loan or lease.

However, having the company claim the vehicle as an asset is a nice benefit as it allows for depreciation deductions. This includes the Section 179 depreciation for autos which can be up to $25,000 depending on the vehicle type and weight. Auto depreciation and bonus deductions change often, so it's best to check out the current year's numbers.

However, you MUST use the vehicle more than 50% for business to claim any Section 179 deduction. The 50% business use of the vehicle applies no matter who owns the vehicle, you or your business. This can be an obstacle for travelers if it's your only vehicle.

If you use the property more than 50% for business, multiply the cost of the property by the percentage of business use. The result is the cost of the property that can qualify for the Section 179 deduction.

One other issue with depreciating a vehicle is the recapture of depreciation or paying back any depreciation taken. I explain depreciation further in Chapter 8.

In the case of your auto, any gain on the sale of the vehicle becomes taxable. When you compute gain here, you have to take the original purchase price minus any depreciation already claimed and subtract that from the sales price. This means if you fully depreciate your asset, then ANY sales price is again!

For example, if you buy a vehicle for $25,000, own it for 2 years and use it 75% for business use, the value you're allowed to claim depreciation on is $18,750 (25,000 x .75).

You take Section 179 depreciation of $16,260 in the first 2 years.

Now the total basis you have in that vehicle is $2,490.

Early in the third year, you go to sell the vehicle and have a sales price of $12,000. Now you'll have to add $9,510 ($2,490 – $12,000) to your income as depreciation recapture.

Unless you plan on keeping the vehicle long term, depreciation is not always beneficial as you can see from the example above. This example is especially true for larger trucks which don't fall in value as quickly as a typical auto.

Would it be better to not have the company own the vehicle and take the mileage? That's something you truly need to think about and do the math to determine which situation is best for you.

Also, if you get into an accident in a company owned vehicle that you are driving for personal reasons, you could end up in a legal battle. The owner of the vehicle is your company, so it might be held liable. This is a huge one to consider as who wants to be caught up in a legal battle, right?

The kicker

The last consideration is a big one. If you own more than 2%

of your company, any personal use of the vehicle must be considered taxable income. Personal use is calculated by taking the standard mileage rate and multiplying by personal miles driven. If you drive a lot for personal use, then this can really add up and will inflate your income.

In the end, this seems like a lot of work for not very much gain, right? You might be an exception to this case, but typically a full-time RV business owner does not want to own a company vehicle. This is especially true if that vehicle is split between business and personal use.

Should my business own my RV?

This is a common question. I almost always will say no. However, there are a few exceptions where RV travel can be a legitimate business expense. Let's go over why I think the answer should be no.

As a full-time RVer, the business owning the RV creates a whole new ball game. You will be required to visit DOT inspection stations since you're now classified as a commercial vehicle. Travel days might become more difficult because you can be subject to searches, weight checks, etc. You will also be required to register and possibly pay higher commercial registration costs for your license plates. You may even be required to have a commercial driver's license. Do you really want all this extra hassle?

Plus, if you live in your RV full-time and have no other property to claim, such as a sticks-and-bricks home, this becomes even stickier. Now you should be able to see why I highly advise not having the business own your RV.

As shown previously, you can use an accountable plan to get reimbursed by your company for any business miles driven. This is usually the best option all around.

To reiterate some key points, business ownership of the vehicle means:

- Company can deduct depreciation expenses of the vehicle (but might owe back depreciation, if it sells the vehicle)
- Company can deduct general auto expenses for business use of the vehicle, like maintenance, gasoline, and tires
- Company can deduct interest on a car loan as an ordinary and necessary business expense (might be hard for a new company to secure a loan)
- Company must hold the title to the vehicle
- Company might be liable in the case of any accident, regardless of the vehicle being used for personal reasons
- As an RV with commercial plates, you will be required to visit DOT inspection stations since you're now classified as a commercial vehicle.
- If the business owns the car, personal use of the car must be documented, and the company must report personal use as taxable compensation on the employee's W-2.

6. Phone and Internet Services

When it comes to internet costs and cell phone expenses, it's not one thing fits all. Does that really exist with business and taxes?

Phone Costs

You can deduct some of your personal phone services on a Schedule C of a sole proprietor business. If you have one cell phone and you determine you are using it 50% for business calls, then deduct 50% of the cost of that cell phone as an expense for your business.

If you have an S corp, use an accountable plan (I explained this in detail in Chapter 5) to reimburse yourself for the business use of these services. You can also reimburse yourself as a partner in a partnership or a sole proprietor. This means moving the amount from your business bank account to your personal bank account and recording it correctly on the books.

Otherwise, have a cell phone plan in your business name and take it 100% as business use. Make sure you can truly justify the 100% of business use though.

As always, you need documentation of business use in the case of an audit by the IRS. I recommend keeping an itemized phone bill to help measure your business vs. personal use so that you can prove your deduction to the IRS. Using a phone bill is also a great way to truly determine how much time you spend on your phone personally vs. for business.

Alternatively, you could get a second phone number and use it exclusively for business.

Internet Costs

You'll also need to split your internet costs just like you do with the costs for a phone that is split between business and personal use.

Let's say you have a data plan with Verizon which you use to access the internet and conduct business. For a few months keep track of how much data is being used for both personal and business.

For example, let's say you use 100GB of data in an average month. You were able to separate out your business data to 40GB of that 100GB. So, 40 divided by 100 is the percent of business use. In this case, it would be 40%. Now you've determined you can take 40% of your data plan cost as a business expense.

Other options

Have two data plans for internet and use one for business and one for personal. Many full-time RVers have multiple plans anyway to keep up with large data usage.

Go to libraries, coffee shops, or other places that offer either free internet or internet for the price of a coffee or bite to eat. Then you avoid the split between business and personal use in your RV.

Is this a legitimate option? For some, it might be. For others, they would not be able to imagine always having to go somewhere else to work. You choose which works best for you.

7. Home Office Deduction

The IRS defines a home office as regular and exclusive business use. This means you cannot use that space for anything but conducting business.

Directly from the IRS website,

> there are two basic requirements for your home to qualify as a deduction:

- Regular and exclusive use.
- Principal place of your business.

In a typical home, a home office might include a 2nd bedroom designated for office use. It can also include a basement that is used for business. A home office cannot include a desk in your living room where you relax in the evenings because this doesn't qualify as an exclusive space.

Home Office Deduction in an RV

Now that you've learned the definition of a home office, do you think you qualify? Is there a space in your RV dedicated strictly to your business?

I believe there are some circumstances where a traveler might qualify. For example, you own a toy hauler and use the garage strictly as an office or studio space. This could be considered exclusive use for business. You also might qualify if you have a bunkhouse that is turned into an office space. Remember, the bunkhouse must be exclusively for business use and not a shared space for TV watching.

Be aware of the rules and decide which situation fits you best. No need to raise any red flags with the IRS, right?

Simplified vs. Regular Method

Beginning with the tax year 2013, you can use the simplified option for computing any home office deduction. Because the standard method has calculation, allocation, and substantiation requirements that are complex and burdensome for small business owners, this new simplified option significantly reduces the burden of record keeping. The simplified option allows a small business owner to multiply a prescribed rate ($5) by the allowable square footage of the office in lieu of determining actual expenses.

The regular method allows for deductions based on the percentage of your home devoted to business use. If you use a whole room for conducting your business, you need to figure out the percentage of your home devoted to your business activities.

A big consideration when deciding between simplified or regular is paying back any depreciation taken when you sell a home or RV. This can add up quickly, so keep this in mind. Depreciation recapture is assessed when the sale price of an asset (your RV) exceeds the tax basis or adjusted cost basis. The difference between these figures is thus "recaptured" by reporting it as income.

Plus, anyone using the regular method instead of the simplified method must keep detailed records of the actual expenses of a home office. These expenses may include loan interest, insurance, utilities, repairs, and depreciation.

Principal Place of Your Business

You must show that you use your home as your principal place of business for it to be deductible. If you conduct business at a location outside of your home, but also use your home substantially and regularly to conduct business, you may qualify for a home office deduction. This can include meeting with clients or customers in your home.

If the use of your home office for business is merely appropriate and helpful, you cannot deduct expenses for the business use of your home.

8. Large Equipment and Asset Depreciation

To operate your business, you need some basic equipment. This could be a computer, a camera, a drone or anything specific to your industry.

How do you expense these big-ticket items as expenses to your business? Typically, larger items are depreciated over time. Let's look at this further.

What is depreciation?

Depreciation (sometimes called cost recovery or amortization) lets you deduct a portion of an asset's purchase price every year until the asset's value to you is zero. Depreciation is based on the idea that assets wear out, get used up, or become outdated over time. The IRS has guidelines for useful life depending on how you classify that asset. It can range from 3 years to more than 20 years!

Keeping track of depreciation can be done with tax software (you'll get a report every year), through a tax professional, or with accounting software like QuickBooks. MACRS (Modified Accelerated Cost Recovery System) is the standard method of depreciation for federal income tax purposes . Essentially, a MACRS depreciation schedule takes into consideration the month an asset was placed into service the first year, then switches to a straight line to finish the depreciation of the asset. Straight line depreciation is the simplest depreciation method. It is a method of distributing the cost evenly across the useful life of the asset.

With one notable exception (Section 179), depreciation is required for most expensive business assets that have a useful life of more than one year and receive wear and tear. The IRS safe harbor for depreciating an asset is any equipment with a purchase price over $2,500. It is fine to sell off business assets that you have depreciated, but it might also trigger depreciation recapture. I explain this further a little later in this chapter. For now, just understand that you may have income if you sell an asset.

If you give away an asset after using it in a business, you dispose of the asset for a zero sales price. This might actually create a loss if you hadn't yet fully depreciated the asset (the asset's value to you is zero). For example, if you buy an item for $1,000 and it has a useful life of 5 years, then after 3 years you give the asset away, you'll get to take the rest of the depreciation as a loss in the year you give it away.

Business assets must meet 3 conditions to qualify for depreciation:

1. It must be used to produce business income.
2. It must wear out, decay, become outdated, or generally, lose value over a period of time.
3. It must have a useful life that exceeds 1 year. For example, according to the general depreciation system a computer's useful life is 5 years, while office furniture is 7 years.

Office supplies do not as depreciable assets, even if they last more than a year.

The following is the formula:

Depreciation per Year = Asset Cost / Useful life

For example, if you buy an asset for your business which costs you $5,000, here's what the depreciation would like over the life of the asset, 5 years (remember the IRS dictates the useful life of assets).

Asset Depreciation Example

Year	Starting Basis	Depreciation Percent	Depreciation Amount	Accumulated Depreciation Amount	Ending Basis
1	$5,000	20.00%	$1,000	$1,000	$4,000
2	$4,000	20.00%	$1,000	$2,000	$3,000
3	$3,000	20.00%	$1,000	$3,000	$2,000
4	$2,000	20.00%	$1,000	$4,000	$1,000
5	$1,000	20.00%	$1,000	$5,000	$0

Schedule 179 deduction

There is also a special Section 179 depreciation which allows you to take 100% depreciation deduction for that equipment or asset in the year it is placed in service. You must have taxable income greater than the cost of the asset to take the full Section 179 deduction. This is quite a helpful deduction for small businesses who need equipment for work. My classification of larger assets is usually anything that costs over $500, but the IRS gives a safe harbor of $2,500.

Remember this special deduction is only allowed if your business has more taxable income than the asset is worth. If the equipment cost $15,000 and the business had $10,000 of net taxable income, you do not qualify to take the Section 179 deduction. Consequently, if the net taxable income of your business is $20,000, you do qualify and can take the full purchase price of the asset.

2019 Section 179 deduction limit = $1,000,000 (one million dollars!!)

This deduction limit is good on all new and used equipment placed in service during that tax year. To use the deduction for the tax year 2019, the equipment must be financed or purchased and put into service sometime during 2019. So, yes, you can take the full cost of equipment you bought for your business in 2019. This includes buying used equipment!

2019 spending cap on equipment purchases = $2,500,000

This is the maximum amount that can be spent on equipment before the Section 179 deduction gets reduced on a dollar for dollar basis. This spending cap makes Section 179 a highly beneficial small business tax incentive, so don't forget to take advantage of this great tax break for your small business.

Bonus depreciation: 100% for 2019

Bonus depreciation is usually taken after the Section 179 spending cap, $2,500,000, is reached. Bonus depreciation is available for new and used equipment.

Qualifying Property

Section 179 was definitely designed to help small businesses, which is why almost any type of business equipment that a company buys or finances qualifies for the Section 179 deduction.

Businesses need equipment on an ongoing basis. Whether that equipment is a machine, a computer, software, office furniture, vehicles, or other tangible goods, it's likely that your business will make purchases during a tax year. This provision is designed to help make purchasing those assets during a calendar year financially attractive to small businesses.

- Equipment (machines, etc.) necessary for business
- Tangible personal property used in business
- Business vehicles with a gross vehicle weight in excess of 6,000 lbs. (Section 179 Vehicle Deductions)
- Computer
- Office furniture
- Office equipment
- Partial business use equipment (must be used more than 50% for business purposes)

These rules change often and sometimes even mid-year, so be sure to keep up-to-date on the current allowances. Remember, the business asset must be purchased and placed in service during that tax year to take the deduction.

Restrictions for Section 179

Section 179 expense is available for any used or new property that you purchase for business purposes during that tax year. It may not be used for leased property, or for any property you inherit or are gifted. Nor may it be used for any property you buy from a relative, or from a corporation or other organization you control.

Businesses that use property for both business and personal purposes may elect to use Section 179 **only if the property is used for business purposes more than half of the time**. Therefore, the taxpayer reduces the amount of any deduction by the percentage of personal use. Make sure you keep records showing any business use of such property. If you use an item for business less than 50% of the time, it must be depreciated and the Section 179 deduction is not available.

Selling a business asset

When an asset is sold, discarded, or destroyed, the transaction gets reported on the business tax return. Any taxable amount (treated as a capital gain/loss) is determined by using the asset's original basis (what you paid for the item), any depreciation already taken, any money you received in the sale of the asset, and any expenses involved in selling or disposing of the asset.

For example, let's say you have an asset that originally cost you $15,000. Your basis is $15,000. During the first two years in service in your business, you take $6,000 of depreciation. Your new basis is $9,000. In year 3, you sell the asset for $10,000. You would have a capital gain of $1,000.

$15,000 (original cost) – $6,000 (depreciation taken or accumulated) = $9,000 (new basis)

You sell it for $10,000 – new basis of $9,000 = $1,000 of gain

If you kept the asset in service for 5 years, your basis would be $0. At that point, any money received if you sell the asset would be considered a gain. See the example below to show the depreciation of a 5-year asset with an original cost of $15,000.

Year	Starting Basis	Depreciation Percent	Depreciation Amount	Accumulated Depreciation Amount	Ending Basis
1	$15,000	20.00%	$3,000	$3,000	$12,000
2	$12,000	20.00%	$3,000	$6,000	$9,000
3	$9,000	20.00%	$3,000	$9,000	$6,000
4	$6,000	20.00%	$3,000	$12,000	$3,000
5	$3,000	20.00%	$3,000	$15,000	$0

Depreciation Recapture

Depreciation recapture is a tax provision that allows the IRS to collect taxes when an asset gets sold or disposed of and that asset had previously been used to offset taxable income. It is assessed when the sales price of an asset exceeds your tax basis or adjusted cost basis. The difference between these figures is thus "recaptured" by reporting it as income. This can add up quickly, so keep this in mind.

The asset that most commonly gives rise to depreciation recapture taxes is real estate. If an investor owns rental property, the investor can use the depreciation of the property to offset taxable income. In doing so, the basis in the property gets lowered. When the property is sold, any gain is computed based on the selling price minus the purchase price and any depreciation previously taken. It's very important to calculate your depreciation recapture liability because depreciation recapture is taxed as ordinary income as opposed to capital gains.

In short, any gain on the sale of an asset becomes taxable. When you compute gain here, you take the original purchase price minus any depreciation you already took and subtract that from the sales price. If you fully depreciate your asset, then ANY sales price is a gain!

Let's look at an example:

You sell a rental property that you bought five years ago for $500,000.

You must add the depreciation expense that you claimed each year for the property. In this example, say you claimed $20,000 in depreciation expense each year for five years, totaling $100,000.

Now subtract the total depreciation expense claimed from the original purchase price of the property to determine your adjusted cost basis. In this example, your adjusted cost basis is $500,000 – $100,000 = $400,000.

Subtract the adjusted cost basis of the property from the property's selling price to determine your total gain. If you sell the rental property for $550,000, your total gain is $550,000 – $400,000 = $150,000.

Subtract the total depreciation expense calculated from the total gain to compute your capital gain (as opposed to your depreciation recapture gain). In this example, your capital gain on the property is $150,000 – $100,000 = $50,000 while your depreciation recapture gain is $100,000.

Multiply any capital gain by the capital gains tax rate and any depreciation recapture gain by your ordinary income tax rate to determine any tax liability. If the capital gains rate is 20% and your ordinary income tax rate is 15%, the total amount of tax you owe on the sale of your property would equal $25,000 as shown below.

(.2 x 50,000) + (.15 x 100,000) = $25,000

If this totally confuses you, then I highly recommend talking with a tax expert or using software to help you compute any gains on assets. It can and does get complicated, so there's no need to go it alone.

9. Taking Travel Expenses

Most of you proudly identify yourselves as full-time RVers, digital nomads, wanderers, etc., because you're living your dream. Consider yourself lucky to travel full-time while working remotely from the road.

However, this isn't the norm. You don't live in a sticks-and-bricks home with a typical 9-5 lifestyle like many. Instead, you have the freedom to roam and be in any state you want at any time.

For some of you, this expands work freedom, and your RV gets used to travel the country following a job opportunity. In the normal lifestyle, many could claim these business travel expenses as deductions for taxes.

However, since your lifestyle isn't normal, your taxes and travel deductions don't qualify as normal either. Who wants to be normal anyway, right?!?!

Can I deduct travel expenses?

The answer is complicated and depends on each individual situation. Here's why.

You're a nomad.

Because of this nomadic lifestyle, the IRS officially calls workers who lead this lifestyle transient workers or itinerants.

What is a transient or itinerant?

The IRS defines a transient worker as a "taxpayer with no regular place of business and maintains no fixed home, each place the taxpayer works becomes the taxpayer's tax home. Therefore, the taxpayer may not deduct any travel expenses."

Hold on. There's more coming your way.

There might be a chance to deduct some of your mileage.

Depending on facts and circumstances, you may be able to deduct some travel expenses that we talked about in Chapter 5. This depends on your tax home.

What is a tax home?

Your tax home isn't the place you live. It's the place you work.

For anyone living and working from an RV, you should take extra steps and keep track of your current tax home. Due to changing travel plans and situations, your tax home may change as often as daily, weekly or monthly.

The IRS gives starting points to determine a tax home based on meeting a certain number of factors. If you don't have a regular or main place of business or work, use the following three factors to help determine where your tax home is.

These factors are:

1. Taxpayer performs some work in the vicinity of their main home and uses that home for lodging while doing business there
2. Taxpayer incurs duplicate living expenses while on business travel
3. Taxpayer has not abandoned the area in which their historical place of lodging and main residence is located; taxpayer has family members currently residing at this main residence or frequently uses this main residence for lodging

By satisfying two of the factors listed above, there is a possible tax home to be determined by facts and circumstances. However, if you only satisfy one of the three factors, you cannot deduct travel expenses because your tax home is wherever you are currently working.

A Deeper Look at Each Factor

Most of the time, the only factor you'll satisfy traveling around the country working from your RV is factor 1. When you only satisfy this factor, travel expenses are not deductible.

This is why I typically say you cannot take mileage between campgrounds or places you travel. You choose to move your home and with that choice incur the cost that goes along with it.

However, when there's a situation causing you to duplicate living expenses for a business trip, you might get to deduct travel expenses.

For example, you need to fly somewhere to attend a conference or meet with a client for work. You leave your RV parked at a campground for this travel. While you are away you stay in a hotel or other lodging. In this case, you are duplicating living expenses and satisfy factor 2.

You'll also be satisfying factor 3. When you went away from your main home (your RV) for that business trip, you didn't abandon your main home as you intend to return to it after your trip and continue traveling. Also, you often use your main home (your RV) for lodging.

Therefore, when you travel on business trips like the example above, you should satisfy two factors, factor 2 (duplicating your living expenses) and factor 3 (not abandoning your main home, the RV), and be able to deduct those specific travel expenses.

To give you a better understanding of how to apply these factors in different situations, here are two more examples.

Example 1

John is currently in Montana for the summer. However, John has agreed to meet with a client in the client's office across the country in Florida in October. He'll be driving his RV to Florida to meet with the client and then continue to stay there for the winter months.

In this case, John CANNOT deduct his travel expenses. Look back at the three factors. John only satisfies factor 1.

He will not be duplicating expenses for this trip, nor will he be abandoning his main home (the RV) at any time. Therefore, since John's situation only satisfies one factor, he is considered a transient worker and cannot deduct these travel expenses.

Example 2

John is currently in Montana for the summer. John has signed a contract with a client based in Florida. They want him in the office for the initial kick-off. Otherwise, he can work from home, wherever that may be. This time John decides to fly to Florida for this meeting and stay in a hotel for the 3 days of kick-off.

This time around, John satisfies two factors, 2 and 3. He will be duplicating living expenses as he leaves his home back in Montana (factor 2), and he will not be considered as abandoning his home because he will return there once business is finished (factor 3).

Therefore, John's tax home remains in Montana as he travels to Florida on a business trip, and he can deduct the travel-related expenses for this trip.

Since your tax home might change daily, weekly or monthly, it's important to keep a detailed record of any travel should you want to consider taking any of it as a business expense.

Lastly, typically an RVer or traveler who maintains a sticks-and-bricks home to return to, but travels on the road for business, does qualify to deduct some travel expenses. Maybe that means you're a photographer and you travel to your photoshoots with your RV, but always return home to an apartment.

Or maybe you're an author who travels to speak and promote your book. By traveling for work you are duplicating living expenses, by leaving, and yet not abandoning, your sticks-and-bricks home. You intend on returning home even though that might not be for several months while your book tour is happening.

How to Keep Records of Travel Expenses

By now you've figured out it's important to keep good records, right? There are several ways to accomplish this.

1. Keep a Travel Log

Keep an up-to-date travel log using dates, locations, and reasons for travel. Many of you might already keep track of places you stay for costs, etc., so this would simply mean adding a few extra details.

2. Track all your expenses

It's very important to keep records of any business-related expenses. This is especially important if you are deducting travel expenses because you are duplicating living costs. You need to prove with detailed records that you are duplicating expenses from where your home is (RV=home) vs. where you are on your business trip. The IRS will request these records in the case of an audit.

Remember to:

1. Keep a travel spreadsheet with dates, locations, and

reasons for travel.

2. Record all expenses accurately.
3. Keep all receipts. (I keep them electronically, so they don't take up coveted space in the RV.)

Tip: Use Accounting Apps or Spreadsheets to Keep Organized

- QuickBooks has a phone application allowing you to attach pictures of receipts for expenses. This saves you from keeping stacks of receipts. This will be a good way to show the business paid expenses with receipts.
- MileIQ has a phone application to make tracking and recording mileage simple.
- Expensify can record expenses with receipts, miles and even time. It can also create a trip itinerary overview if you're flying somewhere and staying in a hotel. All you need to do is forward your reservation emails to an email specified by Expensify and it will show up in your expense reports.
- Spreadsheets

  - Use this for everything from miles traveled, locations, job-related reasons for travel, etc., to expenses and income. I suggest the use of Google Drive, so the data is backed up and accessible from your phone for ease of entering the data on the go.
  - Either use a smartphone for photos of receipts or get a portable scanner to keep everything digitally. Then you won't end up with stacks of paper taking up what limited space is available in your small home.

Duplicate living expenses travel

To sum it up, if you leave your home (the RV) behind to travel for work, whether that's to attend a conference or meet with a client, those expenses will most likely qualify as duplicating your living expenses. Keep records of all air travel receipts, hotel receipts and any meals purchased while traveling. Travel expenses can also include a taxi to get from the airport to a destination.

To make it easier for tracking these expenses, I really enjoy using QuickBooks on my phone. I can enter the expense the minute it happens and take a pic of the receipt to upload in the app. It takes less than 5 minutes, and it keeps all my records in one place. Once I get back home, I don't have to spend time remembering what each expense was for, nor do I have to waste time scanning all those receipts.

Remember every full-time nomad has different circumstances, so make sure you're doing what's right for your unique situation.

10. Navigating Sales Tax as a Business Owner

Whether you're starting a new business or expanding an existing one, here's what you need to know about sales and use tax obligations.

What is sales and use tax?

It is a state and local government tax that is paid by the purchaser for goods and/or services received. Business owners should check with their state government to see if they must add sales tax for any product or service offered. As the owner of a business, you are required to compute sales tax, collect it from your customer and remit it to the appropriate government authorities within a specified time period.

Sales tax rates and laws vary from state to state and even within cities and towns within a single state. Understanding sales tax rates can be extremely confusing, especially if you sell to customers in more than one state.

Currently, the following states do not have a state sales tax at all – Alaska, Delaware, Montana, New Hampshire and Oregon. However, localities within these states might impose their own local sales taxes.

TIP: If you should have collected taxes and didn't, then you can be personally held liable for any sales tax you should have collected and paid.

What is a sales tax permit and who needs one?

A sales tax permit allows you to collect sales tax on behalf of your customers and then remit it to the right government authority.

Except for the states that have no state sales tax (Alaska, Delaware, Montana, New Hampshire, and Oregon), you will be required to get a sales tax license for your business. You may even be required to get one from your local government (city or town) as well.

How to Register for a Sales Tax Permit

In general, these are the basic steps to register with a state to receive a sales tax license:

1. Gather important business info like your EIN or Social Security number (whichever you use for your business).
2. Visit the state's Department of Revenue website.
3. Search or click on the "Sales and Use Tax" section of the website.
4. Click the link to register your business.

Every state and every website will be slightly different, so I can't give exact steps for each.

Here are sales tax registration websites for the top three most common full-time RV states:

- Florida (https://taxapps.floridarevenue.com/IRegistration/)
- South Dakota (https://apps.sd.gov/rv23cedar/main/main.aspx)
- Texas (https://comptroller.texas.gov/taxes/permit/)

When do I pay the sales tax?

Generally, states require businesses to pay the sales taxes they collect quarterly, monthly or annually depending on your state and the business income. You'll file a return specifically reporting your sales tax. On this form, you'll show all sales, taxable sales, exempt sales and amount of tax due.

Not paying or filing on time will result in penalties. Check with your state and local government about the process in your specific location.

What transactions are exempt from sales tax?

Unfortunately, individual states vary a lot on this subject. I highly advise that you check with an individual state government as to which goods and services sold in that state are subject to sales tax.

Generally, a business is not required to collect sales tax for the following transactions:

- Wholesale Items – Retailers and resellers don't pay sales tax on wholesale purchases. Instead, the end consumer will pay sales tax on those items at the final point of sale. For example, if you buy photographic prints for resale you should NOT be paying sales tax. When you make the final sale to your customer of one of those prints, you will collect the sales tax on that item.
- Raw materials – Raw materials used in the production of your goods for sale are not taxed to you. For example, if you knit hats and gloves, the cost of the yarn should not be taxed to you. When you sell the hat to your customer,

you will collect the sales tax on that item.
- Nonprofits – Sales made to nonprofits are exempt from sales tax.

If you are involved in wholesale transactions, you should get a copy of a tax-exempt certificate issued by the state. If you have a retail sales tax license, many times this serves as your tax-exempt certificate.

Lastly, you may find that many states do not require that sales tax be collected on items shipped out of state. Let's dig into this further.

Selling to customers in different states

A common scenario for online businesses and RVers, in particular, is selling items across state lines. This is a complicated gray area of sales tax law and can be confusing.

How do you know which state rules to follow?

Here's what you need to know.

- If you have a physical presence in a state (also known as a "nexus"), you MUST collect sales tax from customers in that state.
- Physical presence includes:
  - An office
  - Any employees
  - A warehouse where inventory is stored
  - Drop shipping from a 3rd party provider
  - Temporarily doing physical business in a state for a limited amount of time, such as at a trade show or craft fair
- If you don't have a physical presence in a state, then you may not be required to collect sales tax. Most states do not require sales tax collected for items shipped out of state.

However, the state you ship to might have sales tax requirements which you need to understand. For example, some states require you to notify your customers to remit use tax on their individual income tax return. This is an area which is still being defined by new laws, so keep your eye out for updates.

This is the general rule of thumb. You should always research and understand any state in which you'll be selling. You don't want to be caught and then owe penalties.

I only sell online. Now what?

This is where it gets tricky.

If you sell strictly online and ship to your customers, you will need to collect sales tax for any shipment in state. If you're still not sure whether to collect sales tax for items, research your specific state. It should have all this information on the Department of Revenue website.

There are many new laws coming out regarding taxing internet sales. The biggest thing here is that usually the small business is exempt from dealing with sales tax of strictly online sales if you sell less than $50,000 in that state. That number can vary by state. The key point here is that your small business might be too small to worry about sales tax in every state you sell unless you are selling over that threshold in EACH state.

If you determine that your business must add on a sales tax charge for transactions in certain states, you'll need to determine which sales tax rate to charge.

Sound overwhelming? Yes, it can be. With thousands of sales tax jurisdictions in the U.S., determining which sales tax rate to charge is no easy task.

If you operate an online business, it's worth investing in an online shopping cart service to handle sales transactions, many of which will automatically calculate sales tax rates for you. An example of one of these services is WooCommerce on WordPress. It automatically calculates tax rates based on shipping zip codes.

I sell a service. Is that taxable?

There are many states that tax services and not just goods. Services that are taxed include design, photography, accounting and more. You'll need to research your specific state to know if you need to charge tax on any service you offer.

As for states that are common to full-time RVers or nomads, I do know that both Texas and South Dakota have a service tax while Florida does not. To learn which specific services are taxed in each state, visit their website.

- Texas (https://comptroller.texas.gov/taxes/publications/96-259.pdf)
- South Dakota(http://dor.sd.gov/Taxes/Business_Taxes/Publications/Sales_Tax.aspx)

Software that helps collect sales tax for your small business

Lastly, there are software services that will help you determine, collect and remit tax in whichever municipalities you sell. But, you guessed it. These software services come with a price and as a small business, these can dig into the bottom line. If you're interested in learning more about these services here are some examples, TaxJar, TaxCloud, Taxify, Avalara and more. Costs for these services range from $9/month to $47/month and higher and depend on your monthly transactions.

The one good thing about these tax services is that many

will integrate directly with your sales platform or accounting software including Amazon, eBay, Shopify, Stripe, WooCommerce, Xero, PayPal, Etsy, etc.

However, if your small business uses a third party platform to sell goods, such as Amazon, Etsy or ebay, it may be collecting sales tax on your behalf. If so, you only need to be concerned with making sure you file and remit the tax with the correct authorities. Definitely worth checking to see if sales tax collection is already happening for you via your online platform.

11. Retirement Account Contributions

Many people overlook setting aside money for retirement and do not realize that setting aside money now for your future retirement can add up to large tax savings.

Self-employed individuals can create Simplified Employee Pension Individual Retirement Arrangements (SEP IRAs) or Solo 401k plans for themselves. Find a brokerage firm and open one today. It is never too late to get started putting your money to work for you.

SEP IRA

The general rule for SEP IRA contributions is 25% of wages or 20% of net self-employment income up to $56,000 (2019 limit). There is a calculation involved with determining your max contribution amount. You'll need to factor in self-employment taxes as part of the contribution limit.

SEP IRA contributions come off of your personal income tax return (Form 1040) and help to reduce your personal income, not your business income on Schedule C. They have no effect on business income whatsoever. If you deducted your SEP IRA contributions on Schedule C, or made and deducted more than your allowed plan contribution for yourself, you must amend your Form 1040 tax return and Schedule C.

Solo 401k

A one-participant 401k plan is sometimes called a:

- Solo 401k
- Solo-k
- Uni-k

The one participant 401k plan is a traditional 401k plan which covers a business owner that has no employees, or an owner and his or her spouse. With this plan, you are able to exclude any part-time employee who works less than 1,000 hours per year. These plans have the same rules and requirements as any other 401k plan.

There are two types of Solo 401k contributions:

- Elective: meaning you don't have to contribute; you elect to contribute as an employee of the business
- Non-elective: meaning you are required to contribute according to the plan created by the business

Unlike traditional 401k plans, there is no vesting schedule for a Solo 401k. That means when you (or your business) contribute to a 401k account you are 100% vested immediately. What does it mean to be vested?

Vesting refers to the ownership of your 401k. While all the money that you personally have contributed to your 401k is yours and will go with you should you choose to leave a job, the terms of employer matched contributions aren't so simple. Employer policies range from three to seven years in order for you to be fully vested or fully own 100% of the employer matched funds in your 401k account. That's where the benefit of a Solo 401k comes in to play; you always own 100% of the company matched contributions.

Contribution Limits

Similar to traditional 401k contribution limits for 2019, you can elect to defer up to $19,000 annually ($25,000 if you are over age 50) of your pre-tax income in elective contributions.

On top of the employee election, as an employer, you can also make a non-elective profit-sharing contribution up to 25% of your pay (based on your W-2 wages).

However, total contributions cannot exceed $56,000 for 2019. This means if you max out your elective deductions at $19,000 as an employee, then the business can contribute a maximum of $37,000 to your account.

A business owner who is also employed by someone else and participates in a 401k with that employer needs to understand elective contributions are by the individual, not by plan. This means you're limited to a $19,000 contribution ($25,000 if over age 50) for ALL 401k plans.

When it comes to making the profit-sharing contributions, each owner and spouse must receive the same percentage of pay contribution; there is no flexibility here as there is with the salary deferral portion of the Solo 401k.

While you can defer contributions to year's end, remember that the Solo 401k plan must be set up before December 31st.

Also, consider there will be fees associated with managing a 401k plan, but these fees are deductible business expenses.

Calculating limits for self-employed individuals

In order to calculate contribution limits for your retirement plan, you must compute the maximum amount of elective deferrals and nonelective contributions you can make for yourself. When figuring the contribution, compensation is your "earned income," which is defined as net earnings from self-employment after deducting both:

· one-half of your self-employment tax, and
· contributions for yourself

As a self-employed individual, you may also elect to contribute to a Roth IRA. Speak with a tax professional to determine which plan type might be the best for your situation. It depends on total income, age, marital status, and business income.

Regardless of which plan you choose to use, it should offer tax savings while investing in your retirement.

Choosing Between a Solo 401k Plan and a SEP IRA

Are you a business owner with a solid net income and the desire to put away a nice chunk of money pretax? If so, the Solo 401k plan is a great option.

Let's look at an example for a self-employed 40-year-old business owner who has $100,000 in compensation:

For both the SEP IRA and Solo 401k you would be able to make a $16,940 employer contribution (.20 X $84,700, which is net earnings after self-employment tax is deducted).

But when considering the Solo 401k plan, the business owner can also make a $19,000 employee contribution. This is where the Solo 401k plan shines through for tax savings!

With a Solo 401k, the business owner can contribute $39,060, which is $19,000 more than a SEP IRA. That is a significant difference in tax savings! Even if you can't contribute the max, any contribution you can make should create tax savings for you.

To decide which plan is right for you, I suggest consulting a tax professional or certified financial advisor.

12. Health Insurance Deduction

Yes. The tax penalty for not having health insurance has gone away, for now. However, many of you might still to choose to have some sort of health insurance to protect yourself in case of a major injury or illness. If you are self-employed, chances are you must buy your own health insurance.

Health insurance premiums can be up to 100% deductible on your personal income taxes which can add up to a lot of tax savings. The health insurance itself might not be inexpensive, but at least you get the tax break from it, right?

Once again, if you pay for your own health insurance, it can be deductible on your personal income tax return (Form 1040). This applies whether you're a sole proprietor, S corp, or partnership. However, the deduction is limited by your business net income.

Also, if you are eligible for health insurance through your employer or your spouse's employer and you opt to buy your own instead, you CANNOT deduct the health insurance premiums. If you're unsure about health insurance deductions, talk to a tax professional to assess your exact situation.

Health share ministry payments do not count for the self-employed health insurance deduction.

Health Savings Accounts

If you have a high-deductible health insurance plan, you may also qualify for tax saving contributions to a health savings account (HSA). HSA contributions are deductible on your personal tax return. For 2019, HSA contribution limits are $3,500 for a single person or $7,000 for a family or couple.

Contributions to an HSA are deductible from your taxable income which can help reduce your taxes as part of your Form 1040.

Putting money into an HSA also will give you a nice little nest egg account for health expenses. Qualified health expenses include dental work, eyeglasses, doctor co-pays, etc.

Sole Proprietor

As a sole proprietor, you take deductions for health insurance costs on your individual income tax return Form 1040. These deductions do not come off your business income on your Schedule C.

Your deduction is limited to your business income.

S Corporation

Let's dive a little deeper into the deduction for health insurance costs for S corps, so you fully understand it.

When your S corp pays your self-employed health insurance, that amount gets added to your wages on your W-2. I know. I know. It sounds like your wages are getting increased by your health insurance premiums. Rest assured this is taken care of further down on your personal income tax return (Form 1040).

Also, know that it is only your personal wages that increase. Increases are not made to your Social Security or Medicare wages, so there will be no additional employment tax owed for the health insurance premiums.

Next, your self-employed health insurance premium reduces your taxable dividend income from your S corp. By this I mean it comes off your S corp income that is passed through to you as the owner, so now you have less dividend income. Therefore, you'll owe less personal income tax.

Now let's address the addition to your W-2 wages. Since you are considered self-employed as a greater than 2% shareholder of your S corp, you get to take the health insurance premium deduction on your personal income tax return (Form 1040). This is an exact dollar for dollar reduction in your gross income.

Let's go over this one more time so that you understand this concept. The deduction and tax benefit of self-employed health insurance is done on your business informational return (Form 1120S). The deduction will then appear on your individual tax return Form 1040. As a self-employed individual paying for health insurance, you should have an entry and deduction on your personal income tax return. If you don't, check in with a tax professional for help on this issue.

Although you get an artificial increase in your wages by the amount of your health insurance premiums, Social Security and Medicare taxes are computed on the smaller amount (the actual salary you pay yourself). Plus, you'll receive a slightly smaller dividend from your S corp, which means you'll owe less personal income tax. Make sense now?

13. Self-employment Taxes and Paying Yourself as an Entrepreneur

Generally, you are self-employed if any of the following apply to you.

- You carry on a trade or business as a sole proprietor, LLC or receive income as an independent contractor (a 1099-Misc).
- You are a member of a partnership that carries on a trade or business. Keep in mind, partnerships must file a partnership return AND each partner files his/her own individual income return.
- You are otherwise in business for yourself, including a part-time business such as writing and publishing a blog.

Self-Employment Tax Obligations

As a self-employed individual, you are required to pay estimated quarterly taxes. These payments will cover your self-employment tax (SE tax) and any personal income taxes you might owe for the year.

Let's step back and understand the breakdown of self-employment tax. You will owe 15.3% of net business income for your SE taxes. This is Social Security (12.4%) and Medicare (2.9%) combined. Self-employment taxes are bundled into your total tax owed at the end of the year on a tax return. This means your total tax liability includes self-employment taxes as well as your personal income tax.

As an employee, you pay half of the Social Security and Medicare taxes (7.65% of your wages) while your employer pays the other half. These taxes come directly out of your paycheck without you even having to notice or think about it. However, as a self-employed individual, you are both employEE and employER. Therefore, you are responsible for ALL the Social Security and Medicare taxes (15.3% of your "net profit").

Currently, the IRS has a cap on income for Social Security. For 2019, this is $132,900. This means you only need to pay the Social Security portion of self-employment tax on any profit up to this income limit.

When considering self-employment taxes, you should consider how much to save and also how much to pay yourself. I cover paying yourself as an entrepreneur later in this chapter.

Keep in mind you must pay the self-employment tax even if you don't have enough income after deductions and credits to owe income tax!

Calculating net profit

Before you can determine if you are subject to self-employment tax, you must calculate your net profit or net loss from your business.

Net profit (loss) = income – expenses

For example:

Business income = $65,000

Business expenses = $15,000

Net Profit = 65000 – 15000 = $50,000

The $50,000 is the amount you would use to calculate any self-employment tax.

Quarterly Tax Payments

Quarterly tax payments are due April 15, June 15, September 15, and January 15 (the following year). A trusted tax professional can help create estimates for you based on prior year income and current year earnings. It's fine to pay different amounts per quarter based on income earned during that time frame.

If your business earns nothing in the first quarter, then you can opt out of the first quarter payment. Consequently, if your business earns a larger amount in the 4th quarter, then pay more tax January 15th. You can make the final decision about how much tax to pay each quarter, but make sure the total is enough to satisfy your tax liability or be ready to pay come tax time.

Lastly, self-employment taxes for sole proprietors and partners are partially deductible on your personal income tax return (Form 1040). Since employers typically pay half of these taxes, the IRS allows you to take half of your self-employment tax as a deduction on your personal income Form 1040.

Anything is helpful when it comes to lessening your tax burden, right?

How do you calculate what you'll owe?

The United States income tax system is a pay-as-you-go tax system. This means that you must pay income tax as you earn or receive any income throughout the year. You do this either through withholdings on your paycheck, usually done by your employer, or by making estimated tax payments.

Self-employment income tax is 15.3%, so figure out any net profit you have and then you'll know how much to pay. Simple, right?

Not quite. The IRS allows for a deduction of half your self-employment taxes. You'll need to take this into consideration when making estimated payments.

Here's the formula:

Net profit from your business X 92.35% (.9235) = business income subject to self-employment tax

If this calculation is less than $132,900, then you'll use this formula:

your business income subject to self-employment tax X 15.3 % = self-employment tax obligation

If this calculation is over $132,900, then you'll use this formula:

your business income subject to self-employment tax X 2.9 % + $16,479.60 = self-employment tax obligation

Personal income tax as part of self-employment taxes

Personal income tax is a little more difficult because you need to factor in any deductions or credits you get to take to know your income tax bracket. You can pay according to the prior year's tax bracket. However, if your income increases or decreases significantly, this might not be helpful.

Here are the 2019 tax brackets to give you an idea of where you might fall. Again, make sure to factor in any deductions or credits when computing personal income tax.

Single	
Taxable Income	**2019 Tax**
Not over $9,700	10% of the taxable income
Over $9,700 but not over $39,475	$970 plus 12% of excess over $9,700
Over $39,475 but not over $84,200	$4,543 plus 22% of the excess over $39,475
Over $84,200 but not over $160,725	$14,382.50 plus 24% of the excess over $84,200
Over $160,725 but not over $204,100	$32,748.50 plus 32% of the excess over $160,725
Over $204,100 not over $510,300	$46,628.50 plus 35% of the excess over $204,100
Over $510,300	$153,798.50 plus 37% of the excess over $510,300

Married Filing Joint	
Taxable Income	**2019 Tax**
Not over $19,400	10% of the taxable income
Over $19,400 but not over $78,950	$1,940 plus 12% of excess over $19,400
Over $78,950but not over $168,400	$9,086 plus 22% of the excess over $78,950
Over $168,400but not over $321,450	$28,765 plus 24% of the excess over $168,400
Over $321,450 but not over $408,200	$65,497 plus 32% of the excess over $321,450
Over $408,200 but not over $612,350	$93,257 plus 35% of the excess over $408,200
Over $612,350	$164,709.50 plus 37% of the excess over $612,350

Head of Household	
Taxable Income	**2019 Tax**
Not over $13,850	10% of the taxable income
Over $13,850 but not over $52,850	$1,385 plus 12% of excess over $13,850
Over $52,850 but not over $84,200	$6,065 plus 22% of the excess over $52,850
Over $84,200but not over $160,700	$12,962 plus 24% of the excess over $84,200
Over $160,700 but not over $204,100	$31,322 plus 32% of the excess over $160,700
Over $204,100 but not over $510,300	$45,108 plus 35% of the excess over $204,100
Over $510,300	$152,380 plus 37% of the excess over $510,300

Married Filing Separate	
Taxable Income	**2019 Tax**
Not over $9,700	10% of the taxable income
Over $9,700 but not over $39,475	$970 plus 12% of excess over $9,700
Over $39,475 but not over $84,200	$4,543 plus 22% of the excess over $39,475
Over $84,200 but not over $160,725	$14,382.50 plus 24% of the excess over $84,200
Over $160,725 but not over $204,100	$32,748.50 plus 32% of the excess over $160,725
Over $204,100 not over $306,175	$46,628.50 plus 35% of the excess over $204,100
Over $306,175	$82,354.75 plus 37% of the excess over $306,175

Generally, most taxpayers avoid any underpayment penalty if they either owe less than $1,000, or if they pay at least 90% of the current year tax, or 100% of the tax shown on your prior year return, whichever is smaller. If you didn't pay enough tax throughout the year, either through withholding or by making estimated tax payments, you may have to pay a penalty for underpayment of estimated tax.

Simply put, you must pay (whichever is less)

- at least 90% of your current year tax OR
- 100% of the tax from the prior year

Saving for taxes

Generally, I advise my clients to have a separate account for tax savings. With each paycheck or contractor payment I suggest putting aside 20-25% into this separate tax savings account. When it comes time for your quarterly payment, you have the money already set aside and ready to go.

If you end up having extra in this savings account, score!

Pay yourself as an entrepreneur

If you're self-employed, let's consider yourself an employee of the business. After all, you are the glue that holds it together, right?

Since you are a vital part of your business, you need to prioritize paying yourself for your hard work just like you would any employee. This doesn't always mean paying yourself a W-2 wage through a payroll service. This simply means you need to pay yourself on a regular basis to support your awesome nomad lifestyle.

It also means you need to factor taxes into the equation.

Pick the best method to pay yourself

Now that you're ready to pay yourself properly, how do you actually pay yourself as an entrepreneur? There are several payment methods for self-employed business owners.

You'll need to choose the best option based on the structure of your business.

Sole proprietor/single-member LLC

As a sole proprietor, the best method for paying yourself a "salary" is to do an electronic transfer from your business checking account to your personal account. This is the simplest method to pay yourself as an entrepreneur. In the eyes of the IRS all money in your business account is yours.

You're free to withdraw money whenever you'd like. I recommend keeping it on a regular schedule as if you are an employee. This helps you budget for personal spending.

To maintain proper bookkeeping and separation of you from your business, it's a good practice to set up separate bank accounts – one for personal use and another for business income and expenses. They can be at the same bank which makes transferring between the two even simpler. You can record this transfer as an Owner Draw in your bookkeeping software.

Think of this as your boss hat writing a check/initiating a bank transfer and your employee hat making the deposit/ receiving the transfer as salary. If you want to have proper bookkeeping, this is the best method to use to pay yourself as an entrepreneur.

Partnership

Paying partners can actually be very similar to a sole proprietor. All money in the partnership bank account essentially belongs to the partners. It can get distributed via a direct deposit or bank transfer and classified as partner draws or partner distributions. Again, a partnership should have a separate bank account and no personal spending should happen from the business account.

I recommend paying any partners, including yourself, on a regular schedule once again. This is to allow all the partners to have personal budgeting for paying personal bills. I think most of us appreciate regular payments.

This doesn't mean you can't take out bonus payments if a business is doing well. They, too, can be classified as partner draws or distributions.

S corp

Having an S corp makes paying a salary a requirement! The IRS calls this reasonable compensation.

Let's repeat that.

A business set up as an S corp is required to pay a regular salary to its owners.

This salary is based on reasonable compensation for whatever work you are doing for the corporation. Think of your title and also your geographical area. If you were to go out and get a job with that same set of responsibilities, what would you earn? Now pay yourself a similar salary so that in the eyes of the IRS, you are running your business in full compliance.

Over the years owners of S corps have come under much more scrutiny from the IRS if they don't pay themselves a proper salary. Because of this, many entrepreneurs face penalties and interest for incorrect payroll tax reporting. Keep this in mind if you're thinking of not paying yourself the proper amount. The IRS may require you to do so in an audit!

If you are confused or unsure how to handle this, talk with a tax professional or another financial expert to get this set up correctly.

For bookkeeping, an S corp will have owner's compensation or wages instead of owner draws. If you decide to take more than your salary out of the business bank account, then you would categorize those withdrawals as owner distributions.

Why the difference?

Because owner wages are an expense to the business and owner distributions are not.

Calculate your salary

Now that you understand you should be paying yourself a regular salary, how much should you pay yourself? When paying yourself a salary, you need to also consider taxes. What's the proper percentage though?

If you calculate taxes throughout the year, you should avoid struggling with a tax bill come tax time. Remember I don't like tax surprises for entrepreneurs. It should be clear throughout the year what you need to be paying as your quarterly estimated payments and saving for any tax liability.

What's the exact formula to pay yourself as an entrepreneur?

THE FORMULA

Profit (or loss) = business revenue – business expenses
   Taxes = 25-30% of profit
   Salary = 70-75% of profit
   This is the simplest method to use. Your personal amount

might vary a little bit from this, but this is a good general starting point.

If you'd like to keep some profits to reinvest back into your business or keep for cash flow in case of a down period, then that formula looks like this.

Profit (or loss) = business revenue – business expenses

Taxes = 25-30% of profit

Save in business account = 10% of profit

Salary = 60-65% of profit

If you'd like to get some tax planning for your personal situation, don't hesitate to contact me. I really enjoy helping entrepreneurs stay on track with taxes throughout the year and avoid any surprise bills at tax time. I strive to help you understand your numbers and how much you should or could be paying yourself.

Seriously, reach out to a tax professional for tax planning! It can make all the difference.

If you live in a state with state income taxes, you'll also need to take this into account when saving for taxes. I think many RV entrepreneurs have chosen tax-free states to avoid this issue. However, if you haven't, you may need to save a little extra for state income taxes.

Let's look at an example to show you the exact numbers.

Let's say your business takes in $8,000 in monthly revenue and has $1,500 in monthly expenses.

Monthly profit would be $6,500 = $8,000 – $1,500

Monthly taxes would be $1,950 = $6,500 x 0.30 (30% of profit)

Monthly reinvestment would be $650 = $6,500 x 0.10 (10% of profit)

Your paycheck would be $3,900 = $6,500 x 0.60 (60% of profit)

If these numbers are similar to your business, then you would pay yourself a "salary" of $3,900/month to cover your personal expenses.

Feel free to use this formula to not only calculate how much you can pay yourself each month but also how much you need to put aside for taxes.

Taxes as a self-employed individual

In the above calculations, I show taxes as a catch-all category. This amount includes your self-employment tax as well as your income tax.

Remember self-employment taxes mean you owe 15.3% for Social Security and Medicare off the total net profit of your business. This is due whether you make enough to pay federal income taxes or not.

Yes. That's right. You may owe self-employment taxes even if you don't have enough income after deductions and credits to owe federal income tax!

I stress this to all entrepreneurs to avoid any surprises. It also makes you aware of saving for your tax liability. As you save for taxes, you should also be making estimated quarterly tax payments. These payments will include your self-employment tax and any personal income taxes you might owe. This is where the 30% of income comes in to play as shown in the above formula.

As you recall, the self-employment tax is 15.3%. The other 15% or so is for your federal tax obligation. This all gets lumped together to form your total tax liability for any given tax year.

14. Understanding Pass-through Income

If you own a business or have thought about starting a business, you need to understand the tax side of the business.

Most nomads and full-time travelers already choose states that do not have a state income tax for their domicile. How does this impact your business?

Let's briefly look at additional details for the most common forms of business entities, S corporations, partnerships, and sole proprietorships, and how income is treated for each.

S Corporations

Unlike a traditional C corporation, an S corporation is not subject to separate federal income tax. Furthermore, most states also do not subject S corps to a separate income tax. Instead, each individual shareholder pays income tax on the portion of the corporation's annual net income received. In other words, in most states, S corps are pass-through entities.

Keep in mind some states might have a "franchise" or "privilege" tax, so it's important to know the rules of the state in which your business is registered.

While an S corp does not owe income tax itself, it will file an informational Form 1120S with the IRS. This filing reports the total income of the business and tells the IRS the amount of income passed-through to the owners. This pass-through income shows up on a Form K-1S which gets entered on a personal Form 1040.

Partnerships

There are various types of partnerships, such as general partnerships, limited partnerships (LPs), LLCs treated as partnerships, and limited liability partnerships (LLPs), among others. Regardless of the type of partnership, individual partners will personally owe state and federal income tax on all partnership income.

The partnership, like the S corp, generally does not pay income tax. Keep in mind some states might have a "franchise" or "privilege" tax.

While your partnership might not owe income tax, it will still need to file Form 1065 to report any income and member information to the IRS. This pass-through income shows up on a Form K-1P which gets entered on a personal Form 1040.

Pass-through Income Explained

As you can see flow-through or pass-through income simply means all the business income gets taxed on the owner's or member's personal return and NOT the business return. Income earned by an S corp gets reported on a Form K-1 as part of the S corp return and is then included as income to each of the business owners. This income excludes any payments as wages on a W-2 and is the income that is left over after all expenses for the S corp are accounted for.

As stated earlier, the business still needs to file a separate tax return if it's treated as an S corp or partnership, but it most likely won't owe any taxes itself. A business or partnership files a return to report the income of any owners, members, shareholders or simply put, yours.

Franchise or Business Tax

Some states might have a "franchise" or "privilege" tax for S corps and partnerships. Check with your registered state to see if your business must pay this separate tax.

For example, Texas has a "franchise" tax for any business profit income over $1,110,000. The rate depends on a service or a retail trade business. Since I know Texas is a popular domicile state for full-time RVers, those who are interested can learn more about the Texas franchise tax here (https://comptroller.texas.gov/taxes/publications/98-806.php)

A handful of states tax the total gross revenues of a company, regardless of the source of revenue. A gross receipts tax is similar to a sales tax, but it is levied on the business rather than the consumer.

For example, Washington imposes a Business and Occupation Tax (B&O) on the gross income from business activities. The rate of this tax depends upon the classification of the business.

15. How to Pay Employees as an S Corp

While an S corp does offer tax savings to some, you must consider the extra costs which are required to be an S corp. These include running payroll, paying Federal Unemployment Tax (FUTA) and state unemployment tax (SUTA), a separate tax return and more complicated bookkeeping. It's important to measure the tax savings against these added costs.

If an S corp still offers you savings you'd like to take advantage of, then you also know that you must run payroll even if it's just for yourself as a more than 2% owner. Paying employees is an important part of any business. But as a business owner, you have additional obligations.

First, you'll want to be consistent with paydays.

Second, you need to keep track of Medicare, Social Security, Federal Unemployment Tax (FUTA), State Unemployment Tax (SUTA) and income taxes withheld for all employees. If you use a payroll service, then it will usually calculate all these numbers for you. These taxes are reported and paid using Form 941.

Federal law requires you, as an employer, to withhold employment taxes from paychecks. With each payday, you must withhold, or take out of your employees' pay, certain amounts for federal income tax, Social Security tax, and Medicare tax. You must also withhold additional Medicare tax from an employee with wages in excess of $200,000 in a calendar year.

In addition, Federal law requires a business to pay its share of Social Security and Medicare taxes. This is the expense of having employees and the difference of self-employment taxes where you pay all of these taxes yourself.

Once a quarter you'll need to file Form 941 to show the IRS your business employment tax numbers. However, you'll need to be paying the employment taxes on a monthly or possibly weekly basis. If you fail to file on time, you will be assessed a penalty and most likely interest on any unpaid amount.

Who Must File Form 941?

You must file Form 941 if you've paid any wages to employees. Once you've filed your first Form 941, you must continue to file a return for each quarter, even if there are no taxes to report. If you've filed a final return, then this doesn't apply.

Directly from the IRS website:

Use Form 941 to report the following amounts:

- Wages you've paid.

- Tips your employees reported to you.

- Federal income tax you withheld. Both the employer and the employee share of Social Security and Medicare taxes.

- Additional Medicare tax withheld from employees.

- Current quarter's adjustments to Social Security and Medicare taxes for fractions of cents, sick pay, tips, and group-term life insurance

- Qualified small business payroll tax credit for increasing research activities.

Use an outside payroll service

I highly recommend using a payroll service which is integrated directly with your bookkeeping. By using software integrated with your books, it becomes super simple to keep track of all these numbers and to remit payments when they are due.

Payroll service companies can do everything from receiving reminders to scheduling payments (most payments are electronic these days) to choosing a full-service option where the payroll company remits all forms and filings without you having to think about it.

Lastly, you can hire a professional to help you out with any of this and to remit payments on your behalf.

It all depends on what you want to focus on and how much you want to handle yourself.

The following are suggested payroll service providers:

· Gusto
· Paychex
· SurePayroll
· ADP

My favorite, and the one I use with my clients, is Gusto. They have the best customer service, are totally customizable to fit your business needs, and will grow with you. Do some research, and decide what service works best for your business.

16. Contract or Outside Labor

If in the course of running your business you use a contracted employee (contractor) and pay that contractor over $600 in a year, you will need to file a 1099-Misc for that contractor.

The Form 1099-MISC or Miscellaneous Income is used to report payments for services performed by contractors for any business.

Taken directly from the IRS website are the following conditions under which your business will need to file a 1099-Misc for contract labor:

> If the following four conditions are met, you must report a payment as non-employee compensation.
>
> - You made the payment to someone who is not your employee
>
> - You made the payment for services in the course of your trade or business (including government agencies and nonprofit organizations);
>
> - You made the payment to an individual, partnership, estate, or in some cases, a corporation; and
>
> - You made payments to the payee of at least $600 during the year.

This is an added bookkeeping and tax item for those who employ anyone to help complete work in a business.

You'll need to file a 1099-Misc regardless of your business entity choice. As a sole proprietor, you still need to do this.

I suggest having any contractor you hire fill out a W-9 immediately as part of your onboarding process. This will ensure you have the correct information to file the 1099-Misc should it be required. The 1099-Misc is filed in January the following year. If you use a payroll service like Gusto, you can also add your contractors there to pay them and keep their W-9 information. QuickBooks also allows you to invite your contractors to fill out W-9 information electronically and stores it for you.

You are required to provide a copy of a 1099-Misc to your contractor, and you must also submit it to the IRS, and possibly a state, by January 31 for any payment in the previous year. For example, for any payments in 2019, you submit a 1099-Misc to your contractor and to the IRS by January 31, 2020.

17. Hobby or Business?

Let's say you enjoy taking photos. Your friends and family are always telling you your photos are beautiful and you should sell them. You open an Etsy shop and sell a few prints online to make a few extra dollars. How do you report this income and take into account any expenses you have for your photography?

Is this a business or a hobby?

Let's first understand that any income over $400 must be reported on your tax return.

Now let's understand the difference between a hobby and a business and when a hobby might be considered a business.

A hobby is done mainly for recreation or pleasure. A business is usually engaged in making a profit and, hopefully, supporting you with income. An activity engaged for-profit must generate a profit in at least three of five years ending with the tax year in question. This means if your hobby is creating profit within three years, you most likely have a business.

However, there are exceptions to this rule. If you can prove you are actively changing up the business to help you make a profit, then you might qualify as an exception to this rule.

Limits on Hobby Expenses

Generally, you can only deduct hobby expenses up to the amount of your hobby income. If your expenses are more than income, you can only take the expenses up to the income amount to create zero income for the hobby. Therefore, you'll also have no tax liability.

Prior to 2018, you could potentially deduct hobby-related expenses up to the amount of income from the hobby. In order to do this, you had to use itemized deductions. The expenses as part of miscellaneous itemized deductions could only be written off if they exceeded 2% of adjusted gross income (AGI).

The latest tax reform (the Tax Cuts and Jobs Act of 2017) eliminated the 2%-of-AGI deduction as part of itemized deductions. Therefore, under the latest tax law you cannot deduct any hobby-related expenses, but you still must report 100% of any revenue from the hobby activity as income and pay tax on it. What?!?!?!

This just means it's important to establish that a money-losing activity may actually be a for-profit business that has simply not yet become profitable. You may be simply do the activity for the fun of it; however, it's important to keep track of all income.

To make the distinction between a hobby or business, a taxpayer should consider the following factors to determine if an activity is a hobby or a business:

- Is your intent to make a profit or are you in it for the fun?
- Do you carry on the activity in a business like manner? Are you keeping complete and accurate books and records?
- How much time and effort are you putting into the activity to make it profitable? Is the end goal to make a profit, to earn some extra spending money or to have fun?
- Do you depend on the income from the activity to support you and your family?
- Do you have normal losses as part of the startup phase of your business or are you deducting your expensive new equipment to create a loss?

- Do you make changes and try new things to make your activity profitable? Are you actively trying to improve profitability?
- Is the activity something you have experience with or are you just learning about this new activity? Do you have advisors with experience to guide you?
- Have you been successful in this activity in the past?
- Has your activity been profitable in some years? If not, what have done to change up the activity to help you make a profit?
- Do you expect to make a profit from the appreciation of the assets used in the activity?

Allowable Hobby Deductions

It comes down to making sure your hobby is actually a business activity. Making this determination will allow you to deduct expenses against the business income.

Within certain limits, taxpayers can deduct ordinary and necessary expenses just like you can while running a business. Remember an ordinary expense is one that is common and accepted in that industry. A necessary expense is one that is appropriate and can be defended for that specific business.

If you're wondering if your hobby can actually be treated as a business, I suggest you talk to a tax professional. They can help you get your hobby in order to make sure it is considered a business and NOT just a hobby. If you're not interested in taking the risk of treating your hobby as a business according to the IRS rules, then simply enjoy yourself and be prepared for the expenses that go with it.

PART III

HOW TO HANDLE TAXES WHEN RENTING OUT YOUR RV OR HOME

Thinking of taking a trip away from your motorhome or RV?

Maybe you plan on staying with family for the holidays or a special occasion like a wedding. Do you plan on renting out your RV while you are gone?

Maybe you own a sticks-and-bricks home but rent it out while you travel.

Lastly, maybe you buy RVs strictly to rent them out as a business.

All of these options are great, but you'll need to understand the tax rules of personal property rentals and a business.

18. When Your RV is Considered Your Primary Residence

Receiving money for the use of a dwelling also used as a taxpayer's personal residence (think of your RV as your personal residence in many cases) generally requires reporting the rental income on a tax return. It also means some of the expenses become deductible. This reduces the rental income that's subject to income tax.

Dwelling Unit

This may be a house, RV, an apartment, condominium, mobile home, boat, vacation home or similar property. It's possible to use more than one dwelling unit as a residence during the year. This may add confusion.

Your primary residence is where you domicile for a majority part of the year. To help prove that you really live where you say you do, register your car to that address. Get a driver's license, vote, and have other bills and correspondence sent to that address.

If you plan only being gone from your sticks-and-bricks home for a year, then you can still claim it as your domicile. Your RV and car/truck will be registered there. You will still be registered to vote there, etc. However, if it goes beyond a year, I would consider moving your domicile state and keeping the sticks-and-bricks home as a rental property.

Used as a Home

If you use your dwelling unit more than 14 days in a year, or 10% of the total days rented to others at a fair rental price, you will have to prorate rental expenses, and keep in mind rental expenses cannot be more than the rent received.

Personal Use

Personal use means use by the owner or the owner's family and includes anyone paying less than a fair rental price.

However, if you stay at the property to complete maintenance work, that time period does not qualify as personal use. This includes staying in the RV to repaint or fix an item broken during rental or to complete other maintenance.

Divide Expenses

Special rules generally apply to the rental of a home, apartment or any other dwelling unit that is used by the taxpayer as a residence during the taxable year. Usually, rental income must be reported in full, and any expenses need to be divided between personal and business purposes. You need to compute the percent of time used for personal vs. rental. Once you get that percentage you can figure out deductible expenses. Expenses include the cost of insurance, property taxes and interest on a loan.

100% Deductible Expenses

Fees for listing on a rental site, hiring a manager to maintain the property, specific insurance to cover the rental period, and any repairs directly related to the rental many times are 100%

deductible up to the rental income you received. This applies if your rental is split between personal and rental use.

If you have a 100% rental RV, then these expenses are usually 100% deductible no matter the rental income. Even if the expenses create a loss, you can take them. Any loss may also be limited by your adjusted gross income.

How to Report an RV that's Split Between Rental and Personal Use

Use Schedule C to report rental income and rental expenses as part of your 1040 income tax return.

If your Schedule A deductions add up to more than the standard deduction, you will use Schedule A to report deductible expenses for the personal use portion of the rental property. This includes such costs as mortgage or loan interest and property taxes.

Special Rules

If the dwelling unit is rented out **less than 15 days during the year,** you don't have to report any of the rental income, nor can you take any of the rental expenses as deductions.

19. When You Run an RV Rental Business

Did you buy a trailer or two to rent out as a business? There are some great options out there to help you find renters such as Outdoorsy, so it can definitely be worth the effort.

However, now you are running a business, and the income and expenses need to be reported on your income taxes using a Schedule C (sole proprietor), 1120S (S corp) or 1065 (partnership). If you haven't already formally created a business, feel free to reach out for some help doing this.

If you've already formed your business, you can take deductions for items related to the operation of your business. These are your everyday expenses that any for-profit business would also incur; the IRS calls these ordinary and necessary to operate a business.

What is an ordinary or necessary expense?

An ordinary expense is one that is common and accepted in your trade or business. A necessary expense is one that is helpful and appropriate for your trade or business.

Common expenses for renting out an RV as a business would include insurance, commissions or fees paid to a service to help you find renters, advertising costs, loan interest on the RV, personal property taxes, phone service to be in touch with your renters, maintenance on the RV, propane fills, basic needs like linens, towels or kitchenware provided as part of your rental, etc.

Generally, you cannot deduct personal living expenses. However, if you have an item that is used partly for business and partly for personal purposes, then divide the total cost between the two. You'll be able to deduct the business portion.

Lastly, a big factor to consider when renting trailers or RVs is depreciation. I explained depreciation previously in the book – refer to Chapter 8 for full details on depreciation, including several examples of how it works.

For a business owner who is running an RV rental business, you'll want to be sure to learn how business aspects such as these can help you in the long run. All of these important provisions are described in Chapter 8.

- Depreciation
- Section 179 Deduction
- Qualifying Property
- Restrictions for Section 179
- Selling a Business Asset
- Depreciation Recapture

Trailers and RVs are considered 5-year property when considering depreciation. Taking depreciation on RVs may create a loss in the first couple of years of your business. That's ok. The IRS considers a loss in 3 out of 5 years of business permissible. This means you can have a loss for three years before the IRS might question whether you are running a for-profit business.

Generally, when I see RV rental businesses, there is a loss the first year or so as you get the business up and running including getting reviews on RV rental websites and understanding what it takes to run the business.

I highly recommend talking with a tax expert about these

important provisions. They can and do get complicated, so there's no need to go it alone.

PART IV
2018 TAX REFORM

By now you all should know about the 2018 tax reform bill, the largest tax reform in 30 years, that was passed in December of 2017. It is called the Tax Cuts and Jobs Act and made some major changes to how you compute taxes.

You may have been personally impacted for the 2018 tax year, but let's understand how they affect you, your business and your taxes. Let's dig a little deeper into the most significant changes and what they mean for you, as a nomad.

20. Highlights of the Tax Cuts and Jobs Act

Tax Bracket Changes

While there are still 7 tax brackets, they have changed. Not only has the tax percent shifted, but the income earned for each bracket has changed. Here are a couple of charts to show the new tax brackets.

Single			
2017		**2019**	
10%	0 - $9,325	10%	0 - $9,700
15%	$9,326 - $37,950	12%	$9,701 - $39,475
25%	$37,951 - $91,900	22%	$39,476 - $84,200
28%	$91,901- $191,650	24%	$84,201 - $160,725
33%	$191,651 - $416,700	32%	$160,726 - $204,100
35%	$416,701 - $418,400	35%	$204,101 - $510,300
39.60%	over $418,401	37%	over $510,301
Standard Deduction	**$6,350**	Standard Deduction	**$12,200**
Personal Exemption	**$4,050**	Personal Exemption	**Eliminated**

Married Filing Joint			
2017		**2019**	
10%	0 - $18,650	10%	0 - $19,400
15%	$18,651 - $75,900	12%	$19,401 - $78,950
25%	$75,901 - $153,100	22%	$78,951 - $168,400
28%	$153,101 - $233,350	24%	$168,401 - $321,450
33%	$233,351 - $416,700	32%	$321,451 - $408,200
35%	$416,701 - $470,700	35%	$408,201 - $612,350
39.60%	over $470,701	37%	over $612,351
Standard Deduction	**$6,350**	Standard Deduction	**$24,400**
Personal Exemption	**$4,050**	Personal Exemption	**Eliminated**

Standard Deduction Changes

The standard deduction for all was increased significantly. Here are the exact numbers:

If you're single, the 2019 standard deduction is now $12,200. If you are age 65 or older, your standard deduction increased by an additional $1,600.

If you are married filing jointly and you OR your spouse is 65 or older, you may increase your standard deduction by $1,300.

If you're married filing jointly, the 2019 standard deduction is now $24,400. If you are age 65 or older, your standard deduction increased by an additional $1,300 for each spouse over age 65.

Personal Exemption

The personal exemption has been completely removed. Prior to 2018, a taxpayer got an exemption ($4,050 in 2017) for each person in their household. This is gone for tax years 2018-2025.

For some, this doesn't matter. While for others, mostly those with children or dependents, this can mean fewer deductions from your adjusted gross income to create your taxable income.

Child Tax Credit Increase

The child tax credit increased to $2,000 per qualifying child. It was previously $1,000.

Who can claim this credit? Anyone with a child under age 17 during that tax year who is claimed as a dependent on a tax return.

Other items to consider to be eligible for this credit:

- The refundable portion of the credit is limited to $1,400.
- The earned income threshold for the refundable credit is lowered to $2,500.
- The beginning credit phaseout increases to $200,000 ($400,000 for joint filers).
- The child must have a valid SSN to claim the nonrefundable and refundable credit.

Itemized Deduction Changes

There are some big changes to the itemized deductions which will most definitely make fewer taxpayers qualify to itemize.

1. State and local income taxes are capped at $10,000. This includes state income tax or local sales tax, real estate taxes and personal property taxes.
2. All 2% above income deductions have been removed. This includes unreimbursed employee expenses, union dues, tax preparation fees, investment fees, casualty losses and more.

You can still count charitable contributions, but they are only useful as a deduction if they bring you above the standard deduction. Many states will allow a charitable deduction if it is not used on the federal return.

Mortgage Interest Deduction

The mortgage interest deduction remains in effect and this includes second homes (RVs qualify as second homes). The big change is that the limit for the loan is $750,000, which is down from $1,000,000. RV loans still qualify, but I'm not sure how many full-time nomads can itemize deductions.

Student Loan Interest

The deduction of student loan interest remains which is helpful to anyone with student loan debt. Make sure to get Form 1098 for the interest paid and include it as part of your personal return.

Qualified Business Income Deduction

This is the big one to pay attention to as a small business owner and a nomad. It's super important and can be very helpful in offering some big tax savings.

Actually, this provision is so important that I'm giving it its very own chapter. In the next chapter, I will go into detail about how it might help you as a small business owner and a digital nomad.

21. Qualified Business Income Deduction

First things first, this new provision, Section 199A, as part of the Tax Cuts and Jobs Act allows for a 20% deduction for Qualified Business Income. There are exceptions and it can get complicated, but to keep it simple, a 20% deduction for running your small business is pretty nice.

In a nutshell, the Section 199A Qualified Business Income deduction gives owners of pass-through businesses such as sole proprietors, partnerships, S corps and even real estate investors, a deduction equal to 20% of their Qualified Business Income.

While this deduction will produce savings for many pass-through entities including real estate investors, the deduction requires some complicated calculations and has some limitations. To understand and begin planning for the deduction, let's dig into the details a little further.

What is Qualified Business Income?

Qualified Business Income (QBI) is actually simple; it's defined in Section 199A as the "ordinary" income minus ordinary deductions you earn from a sole-proprietorship, S corp, or partnership. QBI does not include, however, any wages you earn as an employee. This means that beginning in 2018, as an independent contractor your self-employment income is considered QBI (and thus eligible for a 20% deduction).

QBI includes the profit from an active trade or business as well as rental income as long as your business operates as a pass-through entity. For more information about pass-through entities, see Chapter 14.

This means your QBI includes profits from an active trade or business as shown on a Schedule C, partnership or S corp K-1, or on a Schedule E, and any gains that may occur when a business asset is sold.

To calculate the deduction, add up all these numbers and then multiply the total by 20%. Seems simple, right?

Let's look at a couple of basic examples.

If you have $100,000 of qualified business income, you potentially get a $20,000 deduction.

If you have $300,000 of qualified business income, you potentially get a $60,000 deduction.

A technical point: Qualified Business Income also includes REIT dividends and qualified coop dividends. This logically makes sense since REITs (real estate investment trusts) and qualified coops are also pass-through entities.

What is not Section 199A Qualified Business Income?

Two types of income you might at first consider Qualified Business Income, but that don't actually count:

1. QBI does NOT include reasonable compensation paid to S corp shareholders (W-2 wages), nor does it include guaranteed payments paid to any partners.

For example, you own an S corp with $150,000 in revenue. You pay yourself $50,000 in W-2 wages which gets subtracted from revenue to create your net profit. Now you could potentially take the 20% deduction on the $100,000 profit.

The situation works the same way if you receive a guaranteed payment from a partnership. If your share of partnership profits equals $150,000 and you received $50,000 as a guaranteed payment, you only get the 20% deduction on the remaining $100,000 of profits.

2. QBI does NOT include foreign earned income.

If your business operates outside the United States, for example, you don't get to take advantage of the QBI deduction on any of the foreign earned income.

Note: This domestic business requirement replaces the old Section 199 Domestic Production Activities Income Deduction.

QBI also does NOT include the following items of investment income:

- short-term capital gain or loss;
- long-term capital gain or loss;
- dividend income; or
- interest income.

Limitations on QBI Deduction

The QBI deduction gets limited in a couple of situations.

The first limitation applies if:

1. you're single and earn more than $157,500 or
2. you're married and earn more than $315,000

In either case, you can deduct
THE GREATER OF

1. 50% of the W-2 wages with respect to the business, or
2. 25% of the W-2 wages with respect to the business

plus 2.5% of the unadjusted basis of all qualified property

For example, you have $500,000 of QBI and could potentially receive a $100,000 deduction. If your wages equal $150,000 and you hold no depreciable property, you can only deduct $75,000 because 50% of $150,000 equals $75,000.

This limitation means that high-income sole proprietors, partnerships or real estate investors without W-2 employees might miss out on any deduction unless they have an S corp. Is it worth it to create an S corp solely for this deduction? Well, that's a discussion for your personal tax expert to run your individual numbers. Do consider the costs associated with owning an S corp and the extra paperwork involved.

A second limitation exists where you can't deduct more than 20% of your taxable income after subtracting any net capital gains, but before deducting the Section 199A deduction. Sound confusing?

Let's look at an example:

Say that you should theoretically get a $20,000 QBI deduction based on the qualified business income from your S corp. If due to deductions your taxable income equals $80,000 and this $80,000 includes $30,000 of net capital gains, your deduction will equal 20% of the net $50,000 ($80,000 taxable income – $30,000 net capital gains), or $10,000.

Business Disqualification

Not every pass-through entity gets to use the QBI deduction.

The law disqualifies "specified service trades and businesses" including many of the traditional white-collar professions – medicine, law, accounting, actuarial science, financial services and consulting. It also has a vague catchall for any trade or business that relies on the "reputation or skill of one or more employees."

Therefore, professional service firms with high-income owners potentially might not get to use the Section 199A QBI deduction. Why potentially?

Because this disqualification doesn't apply if you operate a specified service business and your taxable income falls under the $157,500, if you're single, or $315,000, if you're married, threshold.

Furthermore, if your taxable income exceeds these thresholds, the QBI deduction doesn't immediately zero out. Instead, the deduction phases out with your taxable income.

- $157,500 to $207,500, if you're single or
- $315,000 to $415,000 if you're married

If you're below these thresholds, then there's no need to worry about not qualifying.

What if your small business is doing well and fits one of these trades or relies on your reputation or skill?

Let's look further into this.

At first glance, the law says you get disqualified if you earn a high income in a situation where the principal asset of the business is your reputation or skill. The law does not state you get disqualified because a principal asset is a reputation or skill.

Most likely your reputation or skills do matter. However, here's the kicker.

Think about the principal asset of the business. If at least one other obvious principal asset doesn't "trump" your reputation or skill, well, I think you get disqualified.

For example, you're a successful real estate investor with an income beyond the threshold, meaning you lose the pass-through entity deduction. Other than your reputation or skill, what other items could you possibly label as the principal asset of your business? A cell phone? Your laptop? You get the picture.

Now apply that same situation to an independent contractor such as a software programmer or blogger.

This may be a situation where someone through skill or reputation, creates a new asset that becomes the principal asset of the business.

For example, there may be a successful blogger with advertisers who pay the blogger because of heavily targeted website traffic. While the blogger has the necessary writing skills, the asset is not writing at all, but the high volume of traffic through the blogger's website.

As another example, let's look at a software engineer or an app developer. In this case, the developer doesn't sell a service, but a digital good. In other words, a piece of software.

If you're going to take the position that your reputation or your skill is the principal asset of the business, be ready to be able to point out something else that is concrete and obvious as the principal asset.

Other Things to Consider

First, the Section 199A Qualified Business Income deduction started in 2018 and ends after 2025. The deduction, in other words, only works for those 7 years. Tax laws are always changing and being updated or removed, so keep an eye out for any updates related to this deduction.

Second, while the deduction reduces your income subject to federal income taxes, it does NOT reduce your income for self-employment taxes or alternative minimum taxes.

In Conclusion

I hope you enjoyed reading this book or at the very least learned at least one new thing.

Maybe you feel totally overwhelmed or you're ready to dive in, but want some help with it?

No matter how you feel at this point, confused, overwhelmed or excited, I urge you to consider hiring a professional to help with all your financial needs.

An accounting professional can help with anything, ranging from a few hours of consulting to get your business finances organized, to full-fledged accounting and financial planning.

Why do this?

Aren't your efforts better focused on growing your business?

You should do what you do best and leave the tax accounting to a professional whom you trust and is on your side. You deserve to have someone who can be there to help as your business grows.

My Process

To start I will offer some guidance through a quick email or phone chat. I am happy to answer general questions for 10-15 minutes. Through a quick email or phone chat, we can each determine if we will be a good fit for each other. However, if you require an in-depth business or tax consultation, or very specific advice, I'm happy to work with you individually at my current hourly rate.

I firmly believe in helping my clients throughout the tax

process and I'm here to provide education and planning. Together we will work through any issues to help make the best financial decisions for you and your business.

To aid in communication I use a client portal via ShareFile which provides secure, online document exchange and allows for safe sharing of important financial documents. I also use electronic signature software to allow you to sign tax returns electronically if allowed. As you can see, long distance doesn't stop me from getting the job done well, securely and in a timely manner.

Whatever you do, I wish you the very best of luck with your business ventures!

Glossary

Adjusted Gross Income (AGI)

Your income minus certain IRS specific deductions. You use your AGI to see if you're eligible for any tax credits. The lower your AGI, the more tax credits you may receive.

Business activity code

A special code from the IRS that matches your industry. It gets reported on Schedule C, 1065, or 1120S to indicate to the IRS the industry of your business, e.g. a lawyer, an author, a graphic designer. There's a code for every type of business.

Business expense

Any ordinary or necessary expense that you incur to keep your business alive and well. You subtract your business expenses from your business income to get the net profit.

Business profit

The money you make from your business after deducting expenses. When you file your taxes, you must show each type of income that you received throughout the year. If you work for yourself and made money from doing so, you had business income and will have to report it on a tax return.

Child Tax Credit

A credit available to anyone with a child under 17 during that tax year who is claimed as a dependent on a tax return. Starting in 2018 the credit can be as high as $2,000 depending on your income.

Deductions, expenses or write-offs

These are the deductions that lessen your tax burden. If you pay for something that the IRS has decided you can deduct on your tax return, it means you can subtract that expense from your income. Self-employed individuals usually get to deduct half of their self-employment taxes among other items.

Depreciation

A method used to allocate the cost of an asset over its useful life. Terms of depreciation are set by the IRS.

Depreciation Recapture

Depreciation recapture is a tax provision that allows the IRS to collect taxes when an asset gets sold or disposed of and that asset had previously been used to offset taxable income. It is assessed when the sales price of an asset exceeds your tax basis or adjusted cost basis. The difference between these figures is thus "recaptured" by reporting it as income.

Domicile

Your resident state. The state that issues your driver's license and is home to your legal address.

Employer Identification Number (EIN)

A unique identification number assigned to a business entity to facilitate official identification of that business to the IRS. It is used as a tax ID number for the business to open bank accounts, file taxes and more.

Form 1040

The form you'll use to file your personal federal income taxes. A completed Form 1040 will include information on your income, any deductions or credits allowed, a few details about your tax situation, and it'll show how much you owe in taxes for the year.

Form 1065

The form filed by a partnership to report income to the IRS. It is an informational return to show the IRS the profit/loss for all members/owners of the partnership.

Form 1120S

The form used by an S corp to report income of its owners/members to the IRS. It is strictly an informational return for the IRS since the profits/losses are passed through to the members.

Franchise Tax

Just under half of U.S. states require businesses to pay a franchise tax. This tax is imposed on businesses for the privilege of conducting activities in a given state and can be measured in a variety of ways.

Gross receipts tax

A handful of states tax the total gross revenues of a company, regardless of the source of revenue. Gross receipts tax, sometimes called a business tax, is similar to a sales tax, but it is levied on the business rather than the consumer.

Income

The money that you earn. Income is money that you receive in exchange for goods or services. You owe tax on any income that you earn throughout the year (with a few exceptions) including self-employment income.

Limited Liability Company or "LLC"

An LLC is a separate and distinct legal entity from its owner or owners. This means that an LLC can get a tax identification number, open a bank account and do business, all using its own name.

Partnership

When 2 or more people come together to form a business. Each agrees to share in the risks and profits.

Pass-through Income

Any profit or loss earned through a small business that is taxed as individual income. Pass-through income is typically seen in a sole proprietorship, partnership, and an S corp.

Qualified Business Income Deduction

In a nutshell, a Qualified Business Income deduction gives owners of pass-through businesses such as sole proprietors, partnerships, S corps, and even real estate investors, a deduction equal to 20% of their qualified business income. There are income limits and other restrictions, so be sure to read up further on this deduction. However, it can be quite helpful for small business owners.

Quarterly estimated payments or quarterly taxes

These are taxes that you pay throughout the year on any self-employment income. When you're traditionally employed, this is automatically accounted for by withholdings in your paycheck. However, when you're self-employed, it is your own obligation to pay ¼ of your taxes throughout the year – April 15, June 15, September 15 and January 15.

Registered Agent

A responsible third-party designated to receive notices, official correspondence, and documents on behalf of a business. This typically includes tax forms and notices of lawsuits. A registered agent should be in the same state as your business and available during business hours to accept any notices.

S Corporation or S corp

An election of an entity (many times an LLC or partnership) to be treated as a special corporation and pass-through all income/losses to the shareholders/members/owners. This avoids the double taxation of a traditional corporation.

Sales and Use Tax

A tax you collect on behalf of your customers or clients which gets remitted to the state or local Department of Revenue. Sales and use tax rates vary by state, county, and even city, but many localities require you to collect them for goods and even some services.

Schedule A

In order to itemize deductions, you must file a Schedule A with your Form 1040. Schedule A reports medical expenses, state and local taxes, real estate taxes, mortgage interest and more. In most cases, your federal income tax will be less if you take the larger of your itemized deductions or the standard deduction.

Schedule C

When you own a small business, you will need to attach an extra form to your tax return to describe your business; this form is called the Schedule C. This form lists your business income, expenses, and a few extra details about what kind of work you do.

Schedule E

When you own rental property, you will file this form. Schedule E lists income vs. expenses, rental days, property address and more.

Schedule SE

Schedule SE is the form that shows your self-employment tax. You owe self-employment tax if you operate a business or are part of a partnership. This form is usually automatically generated and attached to your tax return.

Section 179 Depreciation

A depreciation which allows you to take a 100% depreciation deduction for business equipment or business asset in the year it is placed in service. You must have taxable income greater than the cost of the asset to take the full Section 179 deduction.

Self-employment tax

Self-employment tax is a tax that you pay on any business

income. Your self-employment tax is 15.3% of your business profit and includes Medicare and Social Security payments.

Solar Energy Credit

This is a credit worth up to 30% of the cost of your solar installation on your residence. This can include panels, batteries, inverters, wiring and the cost of labor to install. This is a non-refundable credit that can be carried over if not used in one year.

Sole proprietorship

A business that legally has no separate existence from its owner is a sole proprietorship. It's the simplest business form under which you can operate.

Standard Deduction

This is the amount set by the IRS as a dollar amount that reduces the amount of income on which you are taxed and varies according to your filing status and age. You can either take the standard deduction or you can itemize.

Tax liability

What you owe in taxes. This is the amount of tax that you are responsible for when you send in a tax return.

Tax refund

Any money that you'll get back after filing a tax return. If you've either paid too much in taxes throughout the year, or you qualified for a refundable tax credit, you will receive a refund. Typically, a tax accountant will help keep you on track so that you won't get a huge refund, nor will you owe any taxes.

Taxable income

This is the portion of your income that you pay taxes on. If you're in a 25% tax bracket, that 25% will be applied to your taxable income, not to all your income. Find your taxable income by taking your Adjusted Gross Income (AGI) and subtracting either itemized deductions or the standard deduction on Form 1040.

Frequently Asked Questions (FAQs)

Should I register my business in Wyoming to avoid taxes?

Short answer. No. Typically I suggest registering in the state of your domicile unless you have a really good reason not to. I also suggest you use a registered agent.

Should I have a business bank account?

Yes. A business bank account helps keep your personal assets separate from your business. This offers separation of you and your business, especially in the case of an LLC or S corp.

Should my business own my RV?

No. The minute your business owns your RV, it becomes necessary to follow all Department of Transportation rules for commercial vehicles including inspection stations, commercial insurance, commercial driver's license, etc. There are some exceptions to this answer though.

If I'm a full-time nomad, can I deduct my RV loan interest?

Yes. If you can itemize deductions on Schedule A, then you can include the RV loan interest as your personal residence mortgage. Most full-time nomads that I meet do not have enough deductions to itemize.

Can I take a home office deduction?

Unless your RV has a 100% dedicated space for work, then you can't take a home office deduction. If your RV has a bunkhouse or a garage like a toy hauler, then you might qualify. You also might qualify if you have a sticks-and-bricks home and solely use your RV for travel to clients or jobs.

Can I take the full cost of my internet and cell phone plans?

For internet and phone services, determine how much you are using your phone and internet for both personal and business use. This gives you the % of business use which you can take as an expense for your business. If you have a separate plan for your business (2 cell phones, one for work and one for personal), then the business portion can be taken 100%.

I rented my RV out. Do I need to report that income?

If you use your dwelling unit more than 14 days out of the year, or 10% of the total days rented to others at a fair rental price, you will have to prorate rental expenses, and keep in mind rental expenses cannot be more than the rent received.

I read that for a 2% or more shareholder of an S corp, the amount of health insurance paid for by

the S corp must be included in the income for that shareholder. Is this true?

Yes. Health insurance payments to an employee-owner are added into the W-2 income. However, they later get deducted from income on Form 1040.

How do you handle tax when you earn income in multiple states?

If you physically work and earn money in different states, then you most likely will owe income tax to those states. This means you'll file multiple state returns. Physically working can mean working as a workamper, traveling nurse, vendor attending festivals, or anything along those lines. If you work from home as W-2 remote employee, then no need to worry about this.

When traveling in our RV to meet clients or potential clients, do we include all of the mileage as an expense even though it's also our home?

If the RV is your full-time home, you cannot include mileage to move the RV closer to that client as an expense. You can, however, take mileage of a towed car or a truck used to visit that client at the office or to a business meeting with that client. If you're driving an RV with no separate vehicle, then the miles to visit directly with that client do count. Again, the mileage from a campground to another campground does NOT count. Only the mileage for the direct work or meeting with the client counts.

What if my business partner lives in one state

and I live in another?

No problem. You each report your own income on your personal tax return for whichever state is your domicile. Depending on the way the business is formed, you may also need to file an informational return with the IRS, such as Form 1120S or 1065.

How do you handle paying state income taxes when domiciled in one state, but traveling across the country?

You may owe a tax return to multiple states or to a state that is not your domicile. In this case, you file as a nonresident for any income earned in that state. You usually don't owe income tax on your entire income.

For example, if you earn income in Montana for being a campground host, but you're domiciled in Florida, you will need to file a nonresident tax return for Montana and owe income tax for the income earned in Montana.

Another example, if you are a blogger and earn income via affiliate links, etc., I usually say that income is earned wherever your business is registered and passes through to you as the owner depending on how you form your business.

How does domiciling in one state and being a full-time remote employee for a company based in another state affect taxes? What if you own a business in another state?

If you are a remote W-2 employee, you pay taxes based on your domicile state or permanent address. It doesn't matter where the company is based. The company should be withholding taxes based on your home address. This is typically why full-time RVers choose no income tax states such as Florida, South Dakota, and Texas.

If you own a business, most businesses (sole proprietors, S corps, partnerships) pass income to the owner to pay taxes. Therefore, you'll owe taxes based on your domicile state. You may also owe taxes to other states depending on where you have conducted business over the course of the year.

How does domiciling in one state while having rental property in another affect taxes?

If your rental property is in a different state than your domicile, then you'll owe taxes on the rental property to the state in which it is located. That income is considered earned in that state.

For example, if you have a rental property in Indiana, but are domiciled in Texas, you will need to file a nonresident income tax return for Indiana and pay taxes on that rental property to the state of Indiana.